Michael 'Pup' Clarke grew up in Liverpool, in Sydney's south west. He joined the New South Wales Sheffield Shield team at eighteen and made his international test debut only three years later, in 2004. He became the 43rd captain of the Australian cricket team in 2011. Michael has notched up 24 centuries from only 97 matches. He has also won the prestigious Allan Border Medal several times: in 2005, 2009, 2012 and again in 2013.

The Ashes Diary

MICHAEL CLARKE
The Ashes Diary

Pan Macmillan Australia

First published 2013 by Pan Macmillan Australia Pty Limited
1 Market Street, Sydney

Reprinted 2013

Copyright © Michael Clarke 2013
The moral right of the author has been asserted

All rights reserved. No part of this book may be reproduced or transmitted by any person or entity (including Google, Amazon or similar organisations), in any form or by any means, electronic or mechanical, including photocopying, recording, scanning or by any information storage and retrieval system, without prior permission in writing from the publisher.

Cataloguing-in-Publication entry is available from the National Library of Australia:
http://catalogue.nla.gov.au

The Publishers acknowledge the trademarks of Cricket Australia in these pages and where used note that they have been reproduced with the approval of Cricket Australia.

Typeset in 13/18.5pt Bembo by Kirby Jones
Printed in Australia by McPherson's Printing Group

Papers used by Pan Macmillan Australia Pty Ltd are natural, recyclable products made from wood grown in sustainable forests. The manufacturing processes conform to the environmental regulations of the country of origin.

To my wife, family, fans and teammates – all of whom play a special role in my success.

Contents

1 Introduction 1

2 Champions Trophy 11

3 The Ashes Tour starts 29

4 The First Test match 57

5 The Second Test match 97

6 The Third Test match 141

7 The Fourth Test match 189

8 The Fifth Test match 233

9 Conclusion 279

Acknowledgements 289

1
INTRODUCTION

26 May. Home.

Here on my bedroom floor are my possessions for the next four months of my life.

My main suitcase contains casual clothes, toiletries and two green Australian cricket helmets. I have three blue cricket coffins. Two hold my cricket clothing, either whites or yellows, and a third holds all my training gear: shirts, shorts, tracksuits. Another green cricket coffin has my first-class cricket gear – bats, gloves, pads and so on – and one-day gear, the main items duplicated in gold limited-overs colours. I have four pairs of runners, each for different purposes, and six pairs of spiked cricket boots travelling in shoeboxes. I have a rack of six Spartan cricket bats.

In another small bag I have some comfortable clothes to change into – we leave for the flight in our team suits – my passport, phone, sunglasses, keys, iPod mini and speaker, watch, personal toiletry items, notepads and reading material. In this bag are also some special items, such as a copy of *Zen in the Martial Arts* by Joe Hyams, and personal messages I've been given. Taped to the inside flap of this bag is a piece of paper that I keep as a constant reminder of my guiding principle. It comes from Mike Young, the former Australian fielding coach, and it says:

> *A professional is* . . . One who competes against the challenges brought before him by others and is willing to test himself each and every day to be the best *he* can possibly be and *not* the best others feel he should be!

Also in that special bag are my baggy green cap and the green and gold pouch that all Australian Test cricketers receive. My pouch is embroidered 'M.J. Clarke 389', indicating that 388 men have played Test cricket for Australia before me. My blazer pocket is embroidered with the number '43', signifying the number I hold in the line of Australian Test cricket captains since 1877. I'm travelling fairly light, but with more than a century of history.

INTRODUCTION

27 May. **Emirates flight to Dubai and London.**

On the flight, I unwind quietly and take the time to think. In the nearly two months since we came back from India, thinking is something I've been doing a lot of.

The first part of the year definitely didn't go to plan. I'd pictured a successful Test tour to India, a season in the Indian Premier League (IPL) with the Pune Warriors, and a good healthy build-up to this moment: my third Ashes tour, my first as Australian captain.

Instead, we lost the Tests in India 4–0. We had some well-publicised problems with team discipline. My back and right hamstring, which had been hurting for most of the Australian season, finally got the better of me in the last of those matches in India, which was shattering as I'd never missed a Test match through injury in my career. And then, as soon as I got home, I was hospitalised with a bout of gastroenteritis. Instead of playing IPL, I was getting over that gastro and driving two hours a day to and from my physio in Beecroft, in Sydney's northern suburbs, from my home in Cronulla, to spend an hour and a half having a machine treating my back, combined with hands-on treatment.

Like I said: plenty of time to think.

I don't accept the way we played in India. There's a temptation to forget all about it – the past is the past and all that – but if you lose the way we lost, and don't learn anything, you'll never progress. What's that saying:

Those who cannot remember the past are condemned to repeat it? We are absolutely determined not to repeat that history in England.

For me, the road back starts with rehabilitating my personal fitness. The sessions with my physio, Steve, on his MedX machine I regard as 'money in the bank'. I sit in position in the machine while it stretches me to full flexion and full extension. Every second I spend in there is strengthening me. The machine weighs too much to take around the world with me, so I have to make the most of it when I am home. We started off with daily sessions, gradually winding back to three days a week. The degenerative disc problem in my back has been with me since I was a teenager, and I know that batting and fielding for long periods aren't the best thing for it – so making my back stronger, when I have the chance, is a matter of life and death for my career.

When I felt strong enough, I went down to Berrima in the Southern Highlands for my annual two-week 'boot camp' with fitness trainer Duncan Kerr, who I've known since I was 17. We did three sessions a day, starting early and ending late: a full mental and physical challenge. It's extreme. I reckon I get six months worth of fitness in those two weeks – more money in the bank. In those hard and lonely hours, I'm not always thinking about cricket, but when I am, I'm thinking that no one out there, *no one*, is putting in this kind of preparation, and when I step onto the field at Trent Bridge on 10

INTRODUCTION

July, I will know that no bowler will have encountered a batsman as physically fit as I'm going to make myself.

When I started out in Test cricket in 2004, some players didn't take fitness quite this seriously. The Australian team had long moved on from beers and cigarettes at stumps, but there were only a few guys who treated batting as a full physical challenge requiring months of preparation. For me, a love of fitness was kind of in the blood. My sister Leanne used to do triathlons and is an aerobics instructor, and I've always loved the feeling of being fit. When I walk onto a ground to bat, in peak physical condition, it does wonders for my confidence. When you're fit in your body, your mind stays clearer. Fatigue doesn't play mental tricks on you. Ultimately, it's the difference between playing that tired shot when you've been batting for two or three hours, and going on to bat for more than a day. It's the difference between scoring 60 or 80, or a double-hundred.

On those drives to and from Steve's, and on the runs in Berrima, my mind kept going back to the tour of India, where it was our batting that killed us. We had the best of the conditions, winning the toss and batting first in each Test match, but were never able to put 500 runs on the board. We batsmen have to take accountability for that. Individually, we all made starts, but we were hardly ever able to convert. At some point, our concentration slipped, and one mistake was fatal. We just didn't have the endurance.

After my boot camp, I started spending three days a week, every Sunday through to Tuesday, at Cricket Australia's Centre of Excellence in Brisbane. I began working on my batting again, and had some good chats with the other guys from the team who'd been coming to prepare. We all agreed that we needed to find out why we didn't succeed in India, and to correct those shortcomings.

There's no substitute for experience, and a lot of our team hadn't played Test cricket in India. In our squad for England, only Brad Haddin, Shane Watson, Phillip Hughes, Peter Siddle and I will be backing up from the 2009 tour; and I'm the only one who's enjoyed the great thrill of beating England in an Ashes series. We're going to have to learn very quickly, and make the most of what we have picked up through One Day Internationals, Twenty20 and county stints in England. It's partly for that reason that the selectors have gone for a more seasoned line-up this time, choosing Hadds as vice-captain and including Chris Rogers, who has scored something like 10,000 first-class runs in nearly a decade playing county cricket.

At the Centre of Excellence, we have been batting on wickets prepared to simulate all the many varieties of English conditions. The ball might swing and seam, but if they have a dry summer it might also turn a lot, as it did in the decider at The Oval in 2009. As batsmen, we have to be adaptable. We've been having a lot of conversations

INTRODUCTION

about how to find our own way to succeed, but there are some general principles. We have to be disciplined at the start of our innings, giving ourselves at least 20 balls to assess the conditions. If we get a start, we absolutely must cash in. This requires a mental adjustment. In Australia, generally the longer you bat the easier things get, because the conditions don't change very much and you can take a few things for granted. In India and England, once you've been in for a while you can't make assumptions about the bounce, the ball and the conditions staying the same. The ball may start spinning more, or it might reverse-swing. Conditions in the UK change radically depending on whether the sun's out, or if it's overcast. So we have to be ready for anything.

I'm confident we can do it. Watching how a few of the guys developed in India, finding a way to make runs and get their confidence back, has me quietly confident that we have some characters who can turn a little bit of experience into a lot of learning.

The bowlers have also been thinking about how they'll adapt. At the Centre of Excellence, we've been working on pitching the new ball a half-metre fuller, to give it every chance to swing. We're also sick of the heartbreak of taking a key wicket only to find the bowler has overstepped the crease by millimetres. So we've been out on the centre wicket at the Allan Border Field, the pacemen coming in off their full runs, practising with a zero-tolerance policy on front-foot no-balls. We're not going to be defeated by these one-percenters, because in Test cricket they become the difference between winning and losing.

It was lapses in those one-percenters that led to the incident in India where four players were stood down from the Third Test match in Mohali. Attention was given to the so-called 'homework' assignment they missed – it was actually just a chance to offer some ideas on how we could improve – but the reality was that we'd been slipping back in a number of key areas for several months, and Mickey Arthur, as coach, chose that moment to draw a line in the sand. He had my full support, and I think the guys responded well.

Of course, a lot was said about Shane Watson being one of the four, and there was speculation about my relationship with Watto. These things tend to get beaten up beyond belief. You can have a difference of opinion about where to go for dinner one night – this guy wants to eat Japanese, the other wants Italian – and all of a sudden they're not speaking to each other! With Shane and me, there's never been a rift or a feud. We're just two different people. In our preparation period, he's had another dominant season in the IPL with the Rajasthan Royals, and I've had a few chats with him while he's been over there. Shane rang me from India to inform me he was standing down as vice captain. If it frees his mind to pile up the runs and wickets, then I'm all for it.

INTRODUCTION

We're under no illusions about how hard this tour is going to be. England have won three of the last four Ashes series and regard themselves as favourites. That's fine by me. We're happy to go as underdogs. We will live and breathe cricket and challenge ourselves to become better players. If we do, we have a chance – a good chance – to prove a few people wrong, and when you win against the odds, nothing tastes sweeter. There will be a lot of things on the field that we can't control, but when it comes to preparation, being ready to handle whatever comes my way, I personally will leave no stone unturned.

2

CHAMPIONS TROPHY

Tuesday 18 June. **London.**

Did I say things hadn't gone quite to plan?

When we left home, I thought I would be with the boys in Birmingham tonight, celebrating a win in the Champions Trophy. It wasn't the prime objective of our tour, of course, but we were the holders of the Trophy and expected to retain it. Then, we would transition to the official start of the Ashes tour, which is our first-class match against Somerset in Taunton next week.

Instead, I'm sitting in my hotel room in London, having spent most of the past three weeks in the hands of the physio. It's been boring and frustrating, and worst of all, I'm not with the team. While I've been stuck here, we have been eliminated from the Champions Trophy in the first stage.

When I said things hadn't gone to plan, our problems hadn't even started.

I guess I ought to begin at the beginning.

After we arrived at Heathrow, we were given two days to recover from the flight, and then three training days. All of this went off without mishap. I did plenty of running, working out the kinks in my back and hamstring, which had held up well enough through the flight. The team had some good net practice, with the fast bowlers gradually building up to their full run-ups.

I felt pretty good, though my batting was short of rhythm. I knew I would need more time in the centre after a break, and the plan was to get that in our two Champions Trophy practice games in Cardiff, against the West Indies and India.

We also did plenty of work, in Australia and now in Cardiff, on our slips catching. Taking our chances is going to be paramount in the Ashes, and we've been working out our best slips cordon. We finally decided that Phillip Hughes would field at third slip, I'd be second slip, and we have a few options at first slip. One of those is Shane Watson, who was playing in the Indian Premier League at the time, so Phillip and I worked on our combination at home before Shane slotted in once we were in England. Trust is crucial in slips partnerships: you need to build a relationship based on knowing, within a split-second, who's going to go for the ball. We worked exceptionally hard on building that intuitive kind of relationship.

CHAMPIONS TROPHY

After the three days of training, I pulled up a bit sore on my right side. I didn't think it was anything that wouldn't be fixed by a couple of days rest. So I missed the first practice game and took that day and the next day off.

The morning of the second practice game, I went to the nets early and took about 15 throwdowns. All of a sudden I felt something grab in my back. The pain was all too familiar. It was the same as in India – essentially the same bugbear that's been with me for so many years.

For the next three days I had treatment on it, mainly physiotherapy and massages and rest, and unfortunately I wasn't right by the time of the first Champions Trophy match. It was against England at Edgbaston, so for obvious reasons I'd particularly wanted to play. Instead, while the team went to Birmingham Alex Kountouris, the Australian team's physiotherapist, decided that orthodox physio work wasn't going to get me ready in time, so he organised for me to travel to London, where he'd located a clinic with a MedX machine. The machine had worked for me in Australia, so we felt we had to go back to that tried and tested formula. Because Alex had to go up to Birmingham with the team, I arranged to fly Steve, my physio from Sydney, to London to look after my rehab.

I had to watch on television as the boys went down to England, not by a lot, but convincingly enough. I'm not a good watcher, and was getting stressed and anxious with every wicket that fell in our chase. The second

Champions Trophy match would be four days later, also in Birmingham, against New Zealand.

My plan was to work hard in London to sort this thing out once and for all. I was extremely keen to play in the Champions Trophy – we could get through to the next stage if we won the match against New Zealand in Birmingham, and then the final group match five days later against Sri Lanka at The Oval in London. But those thoughts were pushed into the background by what happened after the Champions Trophy match against England.

I didn't know anything about what had happened in the Walkabout Bar in Birmingham. On Sunday 9 June, the day after the England match, I went to a fundraising event for the Shane Warne Foundation held to the west of London. Phillip Hughes, Matthew Wade and David Warner had come down from Birmingham to be part of it. We enjoyed the day, and nobody said anything about any incident the night before. I left the charity day early to go back to London to continue my treatment, and the three players went back to Birmingham to prepare for the second Champions Trophy match.

The next evening, the Monday, Mickey Arthur was advised that something had happened on the Saturday night. The team's manager, Gavin Dovey, made inquiries and found out that half a dozen of the team had gone to the Walkabout Bar in Birmingham. Some of the English players had been there too. A wig was floating around in the bar, and Joe Root, the young Yorkshire batsman, had put it on his chin. David Warner had taken exception to this, thinking it was a piss-take of Hashim Amla, the South African batsman.

I found this out on Tuesday morning, when Mickey called to tell me. By then, more than 48 hours after the incident, everyone seemed to know about it except me. I was particularly disappointed that David hadn't mentioned it when we'd been at the Shane Warne Foundation's charity day. David's reason for this was that he'd texted Joe Root on the Sunday to apologise, and had phoned the England fast bowler Steve Finn, who was also at the Walkabout. Steve had told him everything was okay, not to worry about it – and as far as David was concerned the matter was settled. Obviously it served his interests to keep it from going any further.

But it had now. Mickey had decided to put David on what we call an 'amber' level, which means he's on his last warning before serious action will be taken. That information reached Cricket Australia, and they immediately banned David from the next Champions Trophy game and said there would be a hearing, conducted by their appointed commissioner, Justice Gordon Lewis.

That took it out of the team leadership's hands. It all happened so quickly, even George Bailey, who was Australia's one-day captain in my absence, didn't know about it until the morning of the match against New Zealand. Somebody said to him at breakfast, 'What are you going to do about the batting order without Davey?' That was how George found out he wouldn't have Warner.

The commissioner decided there had been a code-of-behaviour breach by David, and fined him effectively $11,500 while standing him down from the remaining Champions Trophy games and our two Ashes warm-up fixtures against Somerset and Worcestershire. It was a stern punishment, as it jeopardised David's prospects of playing in the First Test match, considering he wouldn't have played any cricket by then for four weeks. That in turn would affect his chances for the Second Test match, which will be back-to-back with the first.

David had already been censured during the IPL for some intemperate remarks on Twitter directed at the News Limited journalists Malcolm Conn and Robert Craddock. I was surprised that he would lose his cool in a bar for no good reason. I felt that there had to be more to it. I was also disappointed that the boys would be out in the early hours of the morning when they had just lost a game. I'm all for having a good night as a team to celebrate, but pick your night to celebrate a win – don't go out and have a laugh with some England players after losing to them. It just wasn't acceptable.

In London, I was working hard on my routine with Steve, spending three to four sessions a day on the MedX machine. Under his care, my back improved dramatically.

Our results didn't. We got into a good position against New Zealand, but rain blew in and washed the game out before we could get a result. That was a real shame, because a win would have pepped us up. I willed the rain to stay away. But it wasn't to be.

That day, I had a series of cortisone injections: two in my facet joints, one nerve root injection through the right glute, and one injection into the muscle area above the L4 and L5 vertebrae.

I could immediately feel a benefit from the injections and the MedX and physio treatment, so I was in a better mood when the Champions Trophy squad came down to London. One of my first priorities was to sit down with David for an hour. I wanted to hear the full story from him, just between the two of us, teammate to teammate rather than in the setting of a formal disciplinary hearing. I made my thoughts clear about how disappointed I was that he hadn't told me when he'd seen me on the Sunday. I could understand (but not agree with) him not wanting it to get out, but his actions had been unacceptable for an Australian Test cricketer. It wasn't me he'd let down, though: he'd let down his team, his family, and most importantly himself. Our standards had been slipping in a number of ways – small things that add up to big things – and he knew that. I really think David has a big future in Australian cricket. Of course he can overcome this obstacle, but he has to start now.

Anyway, he'd been punished. Any time you get dropped for a game is the harshest sanction for a proud cricketer.

Another priority was to catch up with Shane Watson. In the last few days I've received phone calls from guys in the one-day squad and from staff referring to Shane's attitude around the group. Shane has strong opinions, which is his right as a senior member of the team, but sometimes there's a right way and a wrong way to put them. I wanted to know if everything was okay with him, to hear how he was feeling in his own words, rather than through others. I didn't want people talking about anybody in the team behind their back. Whatever I heard, I wanted to hear from Shane himself, so that I could help.

We've had honest conversations, which is fantastic. We've had to do this before, in India. Before the First Test in Chennai, I called Watto into my room for an hour and a half. We got a lot of things off our chests and thrashed it out and I think that from that point our relationship has been extremely good. My aim is to have us all going in the same direction. In these situations, the worst thing is when you hear things second- or third-hand. As in Chennai, I feel that when we have these talks, we come out of it as a stronger team.

The boys went out at the Oval yesterday and lost to Sri Lanka. Their assignment was extremely difficult. Because of the wash-out against New Zealand, they had to win the match by a massive margin. They showed a lot of character trying their best to achieve that, but couldn't manage it. So we're out of the Champions Trophy.

James Sutherland, chief executive of Cricket Australia, and Pat Howard, our team performance manager, have come over for a number of meetings. James was pretty ropable about the Warner matter.

We have four days to cool our heels in London before we catch a bus over to Taunton to meet the guys from the Australia A team who have been touring Scotland and England, and get our Ashes tour properly started.

I can't wait.

Friday 21 June. **London.**

Today I had a full cricket training session for the first time in three weeks. I feel like cracking the champagne. It feels like it's been a long road back. It isn't, really, but all the frustrations of not being in the Champions Trophy and dealing with those team issues have added to my impatience to get back on the field and contribute as a player.

Alex has been steering me through it, bit by bit. Since the injections, everything seems to have been holding up. In the past two weeks, I haven't been totally immobile. I started with some tennis ball throwdowns, batting gently for a few minutes at a time. That progressed to cricket ball throwdowns. The next step was some low-intensity net batting in full gear against local net bowlers. Today it was facing our bowlers in the nets. I batted for 45 minutes in three 15-minute sessions, then had 15 minutes of throwdowns and 20 minutes of slips catching.

If I had to play a Test match starting today, I'd be ready. Yes! I can feel the excitement building. Our practice sessions have been at local school grounds so far, where they have fabulous facilities. On Sunday, for the first time, we go to Lord's for our practice. Then on Monday we hop on the bus to Taunton and meet the Australia A boys – Brad Haddin, Usman Khawaja, James Pattinson, Peter Siddle, Ashton Agar, Nathan Lyon, Ryan Harris, Steve Smith and Jackson Bird. With the Champions Trophy guys and Eddie Cowan and Chris Rogers, who've been playing county cricket, that brings the whole Ashes squad together. At last!

I've been thinking about the Champions Trophy result, which was certainly disappointing. But aside from the guys who were only here for that tournament, I would say that the players' real focus has been on the Ashes. Not that that's an excuse for the way we played, but I don't think our minds were fully switched on for that event. If it had been outside England, it might have been different. But when I got here and gave press conferences, nine out of ten questions I was asked were about the Ashes.

It has been the same with all our planning and conversations. This is an Ashes tour. At the Centre of

Excellence in Brisbane, for instance, we were using red Dukes balls 90 per cent of the time, as they use in Test cricket in England.

In the batting group, we've done a lot of talking, because we know that our performance is going to be the key. Everyone talks about how much talent our bowlers have, but if the batsmen don't make enough runs, the bowlers will never be talented enough to win the games for us. Runs on the board are what we need. We have to improve quickly on our performance in India, and our focus has been on getting our defences right. Throughout my career, I've seen my defence as my go-to. We have to build the foundations of our innings patiently. That doesn't mean being negative – I don't want guys to be going out and blocking for 50 overs, then getting out for 20 runs. You can show as much positive intent in good defence as you can by smacking fours. It's about taking control of the situation, and showing the bowlers that you're in charge. The best way to do that in Test cricket is by building an impregnable defence.

Saturday 22 June. **London. Afternoon.**

Days of ordinary training feel precious to me, after all the time in rehab. One thing an injury does is stop you from taking anything for granted.

I had an early start and some treatment from Alex, before a one-hour coach ride to practice. The rain was closing in, and we hustled along to fit in as much work as possible. At our lunch break, we sat down and watched 20 minutes of the first rugby Test between the Wallabies and the British and Irish Lions in Brisbane. It was fun to take our minds off cricket, and the match was very close, but the Wallabies missed a couple of penalty goal shots in the last few minutes and didn't get the result we all wanted.

Back at the hotel, I had some more treatment from Alex before the two of us took a good long walk in Hyde Park. We discussed how far I'd come with my improvement, and what we needed to do from here. It's more or less a matter of walking that fine line between committing myself fully to the important cricket fixtures, but not overdoing it when I feel the warning signs. Tomorrow we're at Lord's, the first time on that beautiful ground, and looking forward to training well.

I have to say, it's great to be back in action, and I can't wait until we play in Taunton.

Saturday 22 June. **London. Night.**

I don't know if I'm going to sleep tonight. I'm in complete turmoil.

During the afternoon, I'd passed by James and Pat as they were coming in and out of meetings. They'd each said, separately, 'We need to have a chat', but they hadn't set a time.

Early in the evening, my wife Kyly and I were having a drink in the bar of the team hotel, the Royal Garden in Kensington, before going out to dinner. As we were walking out, we crossed paths with James and Pat.

'Do you guys want to see me?' I asked.

'Sure. How about now?'

I told them that Kyly and I had a dinner booking, but I'd be free afterwards.

'Okay,' James said. 'Go to dinner and we'll meet back here later.'

When we returned to the hotel just after 8.30 pm, Kyly went up to our room and I sat in the bar by myself. James and Pat soon came in.

Among the things I expected to talk about, one was the possibility of calling in players from outside the official Ashes squad. Mickey and I were keen on bringing in Steve Smith after his good form on the Australia A tour.

I've been finding it stressful lately to be both captain and selector. Until tonight, I've been a member of the National Selection Panel (NSP), one of the recommendations of the Argus Review in 2011. It had also recommended making the coach a part of a five-man panel. This was also the time I'd taken over the national captaincy from Ricky Ponting, so during my entire tenure as captain I've also been a selector.

But after the Indian tour, I wrote an email to James and Pat offering to resign as a selector. I'd grown increasingly uncomfortable with that role over the whole period. I felt being a selector was a full-time job that I couldn't keep up with. As for players inside the team, I felt my time was better used in one-on-one chats and helping them at training, having coffee or breakfast or other off-field get-togethers with them, rather than talking about them with selectors. It can stretch the bond between me and that player when I'm part of a selection committee that might be considering his position. I can't break selection-table confidentiality, so I have to support every decision, but on the other hand I have a personal relationship with that teammate. It's a very complicated situation, and does nothing to build trust between the boys and me.

I thought it was a good time to get on the front foot and tell Cricket Australia I wanted to step down from the panel. However, while listening to my concerns, they didn't accept my resignation. They said it wasn't the right time. I accepted that, and just cracked on.

At any rate, tonight I thought we'd be talking about bringing in Smithy and various other matters. Instead, I was blind-sided.

James spoke. 'Tomorrow we're going to Bristol to let Mickey know that he's no longer required as our head coach, and we're going to offer Darren Lehmann the job.'

My head went so light that I thought I was going to fall off my stool. I was too stunned to speak. In the end, I think the first thing I said was, 'I don't know what to say.' It was the last thing – the absolute last thing – I thought the meeting was going to be about.

James and Pat talked on a bit while I calmed down. We had a drink, and I tried to take it in. They know how close I am to Mickey, and how much work has gone into planning for this series.

'We wanted you to be the first to know,' James said. 'So how do you feel about it? How will the team handle it?'

I wasn't thinking about myself. I just said, 'Mickey's going to be shattered.'

'How about the team?'

My concern for the team, I said, was in the timing of the decision. Did it have to be now? The First Test was starting in 18 days. Leaving aside the merits or otherwise of the decision, what kind of signal did it send to replace the coach four weeks into an England tour, 18 days before an Ashes series started?

'Are you sure it's the right time?' I said. 'We've done so much planning together for this series.' And that was leaving aside what message it would send our opponents. The English would make the most of this and see it as a sign of panic, that's for sure.

James and Pat spoke about what they thought Darren could bring to the table. I was still trying to get over the shock. They felt that the team's results in India and now in the Champions Trophy confirmed that Mickey's coaching style wasn't getting the on-field results we were looking for. The off-field problems, in India and England, also didn't seem to be getting better.

As far as I was concerned, it was ourselves, the players, who had not performed well enough in India.

'Also,' James said, 'we're happy to accept your resignation as a selector now.'

I was so shocked about Mickey, I barely even heard him.

Two hours later, I drifted up to my room, where I am now. Since I've been up here, the shock hasn't worn off, and now there is guilt too. Mickey and I have been talking on the phone several times a day about the Australia A team and the possible selection of the Test squad. He has just rung me, and when I saw his number come up I didn't take his call. I don't want to lie to him. I know that his mother's very sick as well, and may not live for much longer. The timing could never have been good for this decision, but it could hardly have been worse.

Mickey's a very caring guy. A coach has to be the bad cop sometimes, and that's what Mickey has found most difficult. He and I have complemented each other, and I see him as a kind, fatherly figure around the team, but there have been times when Cricket Australia have spoken to him about the coach's need to be tougher on team discipline.

My head is spinning. Tomorrow I have to speak to him. I won't be sleeping much tonight.

Sunday 23 June. **London.**

I've spoken to Mickey this morning. He texted me as soon as he'd got the news from Pat, who drove to Bristol first thing to tell him face-to-face. I told him how terrible I felt for him, and said how much we, the players, felt for him. He, as always, is taking it stoically.

The hardest part is how I feel for him as a man. This has happened to him while his mother, who is in South Africa, is not far from passing away. I want to be there, emotionally, to support him. But I'm also part of the system that is now letting him go. He's being very encouraging to us, and is telling me that we can win the Ashes. He really feels we're on the cusp of great things, and he wants to see us achieve our potential. I still can't believe he's not going to be on this journey with us.

3

THE ASHES TOUR STARTS

Monday 24 June. Taunton.

What a way to start the Ashes tour proper. As Pat Howard drove me from Bristol to Taunton, about a three-hour trip, I had time to let it all sink in. The thing is, I have to look ahead. People come and go, the game moves forward, and you've got to get on with it. It's the same for a head coach as it is for a player. We've seen it with Ricky Ponting and Mike Hussey when they retired, and all the other players who get dropped. Individuals go, but those who are left have the responsibility to keep carrying the game forward. One day it'll be me who goes. It's brutal, but that's just the way it is.

One of the first things I did in Bristol was to tell the team that if they wanted to talk to Mickey and say goodbye, or send him any other message, now was the time. Nearly all of them saw him personally.

While the team travelled to Taunton, I stayed in Bristol for a press conference. First up were James and Pat explaining the decision, then Mickey said his piece, and finally Darren Lehmann and me. It was quite awkward for Darren and Mickey. They have no personal vendettas against each other. They're both very nice men, and while it was no doubt excruciating for them, they handled it in the manner I'd have expected.

While we were waiting for our press conference, Darren and I sat down and had a coffee. We had a good chat about things. He was as shocked as anybody by Mickey's sacking, and was put on the spot when James and Pat asked him to take over. He said yes, because that's the type of guy Boof is – always up for a challenge.

We know each other very well. He was in the Australian team when I made my Test debut on the tour of India in 2004. It was a great tour, Australia's First Test series win in India since 1969, and I got to know Boof extremely well. I loved every minute I played with him. While Ricky Ponting and Adam Gilchrist were the captain and vice-captain, for me, as a young guy, the informal team leaders were guys like Boof, Glenn McGrath, Shane Warne, Justin Langer and Damien

Martyn. I loved talking cricket with them. I dare say I'll have a lot more time to do that with Darren now. He's a great man. We have a lot of common themes as players. Boof was positive and aggressive, and liked facing spin bowling. He's a big team man, as was evident in 2004 when he said publicly that if the selectors had to choose between him and a young player, all other things being equal, he would go for the younger player. I don't know if the selectors actually did make that choice. But if they did, the younger player in question was me.

The best thing is, he has total confidence that we can win. He knows it's going to be a tough challenge, but when I look into his eyes and say, 'If we play our best we can win the Ashes', I can see that he agrees with me.

I'm looking forward to having him as head coach.

Tuesday 25 June. **Taunton.**

Today we had our first training session with Boof, and it went really well. When James and Pat asked me how the team would respond to the change, I suppose there was one thing that went without saying: Darren has the players' respect. Respect is a huge thing in this group, and has been for as long as I've been playing. You have to earn it, but once you've got it, you have it unconditionally. Boof can walk into the room and he already has that respect because of how good a player he was. On top of that, a lot of the boys know him as a coach, whether at Queensland, the Brisbane Heat, or in the last few weeks with Australia A. He's starting off with a lot of advantages.

Tonight, in a great way to inject a lighter note into what's been an intense and dramatic few days, we had a team trivia night and dinner. Peter Brukner, our team doctor, ran it, as usual. Each person in the team and support staff had to write down a fact about themselves that nobody else would know. Those facts were then laid out alongside a list of everyone's names. The job was to fit the facts together with the names.

We did it in pairs, and Peter paired me up with Phillip Hughes. Now, Hughesy is always copping stick from the boys because he's from the country and they reckon he's not exactly a pillar of academic learning. Hughesy knows a lot about cattle and cricket. And he says he may not be able to spell very well, but he's 'street smart'. Whenever he says that, he only gets more chuckles. But anyway, he had the last laugh tonight: Hughesy and I came out as winners. We were all in good spirits. I know he certainly is, after shutting a few people up.

I'm still reeling a bit from the Mickey thing, though. Today I got a message from him: his mother had passed away in South Africa. It's been a heartbreaking 24 hours for him.

Nothing more I can say, but I'm going to keep supporting him as best I can.

I've always been able to turn to my family in difficult times, and my nephew Byron's second birthday gave me a chance to call him, have a chat to my sister, and reconnect with their lives.

Wednesday 26 June. **Taunton.**

Today is my dad's birthday, so I gave him a call. He's about to go into hospital for a knee replacement, so I guess he won't be celebrating too hard.

We had an interesting day's cricket, I guess the type of play that happens when you're rusty and getting into shape. I lost the toss – a bad move on a ground which has just about the best batting wicket in the country and a small, fast outfield. We bowled too wide with the new ball, and let Nick Compton, who's just learnt that he's been dropped from the England team, take out some of his frustration. Then, through the middle of the day, we bowled too short and both sides of the stumps. It wasn't great, and Somerset got to 2/304 by the time we were getting ready to take the second new ball.

James Faulkner got a breakthrough in the last over with the old ball, and then Mitchell Starc and Jimmy Pattinson got it totally right, and showed what a destructive force they can be when they get on a roll. In six overs with the second new ball, they took seven wickets for ten runs. It's a great feeling in the field when the wickets tumble like this, and we walked off on a bit of a high after turning a pretty ordinary day into a good one.

But the lessons remain to be learnt. When the sun's out, we have to attack the stumps early. Later, when the ball gets old and batting gets easier, we have to bowl with more discipline and apply pressure. And then, when things turn our way, we have to cash in.

Thursday 27 June. Taunton.

We've had a good day's batting, albeit shortened by some light but persistent rain that kept us off the field in the afternoon. For me, it's hard to believe, but this has been my first bat on tour. We've been here a month, and finally I've padded up and faced opposition bowlers in a match situation.

The funny thing is, even after nine years as an international cricketer, I get just as nervous going in to bat in a game like this as in a Test match. Even if it's club cricket for Western Suburbs in Sydney, I'm still like a cat on a hot tin roof while I'm waiting to bat. I can't sit down, and pace back and forth in the dressing room, listening to music on my iPod. When I go out into the middle, I'm so tense all I want to do is get off the mark. I wish I wasn't like this, but I am. It's not going to change now. I guess if I'm serious, I have to acknowledge that my nerves are a measure

THE ASHES TOUR STARTS

of my hunger to score runs, and my excitement to be in a cricket match. It's no different now from when I was a kid. And if it fades away, maybe that's when I should be thinking of a new career. Right now, because of the enforced lay-off and all the physio treatment, my excitement is as high as it's ever been.

I just wanted to play solidly, and more or less achieved that with 45 runs in two hours before I nicked one. All in all, a pretty satisfying knock.

The batting highlight was Watto's 90 at the top of the order. I batted with him for about 15 overs and he was hitting the ball as hard as ever. Watto going back to the opening slot has been getting a lot of press, since Boof announced the move before this game. It's been well documented for about a year that Watto has wanted to open the batting for Australia. This has made it hard for Ed Cowan and David Warner, who became the openers in 2011–12 while Watto was out with an injury. When he came back into the team, Ed and David were going so well that Watto had to slot in at number four. He hasn't had a great run there, and everyone knows, when they look at his figures, that his biggest impact as a Test batsman has been when he's played against the new ball – as he does in one-day and Twenty20 cricket.

What's confused people a bit is that Darren Lehmann was the one who told the media, during the practice match in Somerset that Watto would be opening the batting in the Test matches. They then ran with the story that Boof had come in and decided to give Watto what he'd been asking for.

This wasn't the case. Now that I'm not a selector, the NSP will give me a team at Trent Bridge in the lead-up to 10 July and *I'll* decide who bats where. Since I've played for Australia, the captain has always chosen the batting order. On the matter of Watto individually, over the past three months Mickey and I have had a lot of communication with him. I've talked to Watto, and other players, about the roles I see them playing in the Ashes series, and they've talked to us about what they want. This has been an ongoing process, and Darren has slipped into that smoothly. We've had ideas for a while that Watto might be the best guy to start the Ashes series opening the batting, but also, the best batting order is going to vary with the conditions in each innings, so it's something we'll be constantly working on.

Friday 28 June. **Taunton.**

Everything on the field went pretty much to plan today. Phillip Hughes batted extremely well to make 76 not out. For a guy who's played most of his cricket as an opener, he has adapted brilliantly to batting in the Australian team at number three and now, potentially, in the middle order.

Our goal was to get past Somerset's total quickly and

declare, then bowl to try to force a result. It's not that there are any first-innings points at stake, but you always like to get that 'win'.

With the ball, Jimmy Pattinson and Mitchell Starc led the way, and Nathan Lyon bowled pretty well to take three wickets. We got Somerset out for 260, leaving ourselves eight overs plus a day to run down that total. I feel that it's important to balance the need of individual players to get practice and push for a Test place against the wish to win the match. Ed Cowan and Usman Khawaja, who didn't get much batting in the first innings, have opened, while Watto will take a rest and come in later if needed. We'd all really like a win, not having won a match since before the tour of India. It would be a nice way to top the game off tomorrow.

At home, Dad's just come out of knee replacement surgery. We've been on the phone, and he sounds like he's in a bit of pain, but the doctors have said the operation seems to have gone well. I hope I'm not looking at my own future there.

Saturday 29 June. **Worcester.**

It was a boost, and also a relief, to get out of Taunton with a fairly comfortable six-wicket win. It doesn't matter who the opposition is, if it's first-class cricket, chasing down a decent fourth-innings total is a challenge. Ed,

Usman and Hughesy all played well at the top, I had another bat and made 26, and then Brad Haddin went out and tidied things up with a quick half-century.

What pleased me most was that everyone played a part in the win. All the batsmen got some runs and the bowlers did well. Our attitude and intent were outstanding, playing to win and attacking to take wickets. All in all, it was a very good performance.

Straight after the game, we had a two-hour bus ride to Worcester. There was a good feeling in the group, some beers flowing on the bus to celebrate our first win.

Tonight we're all going out in Worcester as a team. As I said after the business in Birmingham, I'm all for celebrating, but a drink tastes a lot better when you've had a win.

Sunday 30 June. **Worcester.**

As feared, my inbox was chockers, with 60 unanswered emails. I've had to spend the day calling family and friends, catching up on everything I missed while we were in Taunton. Luckily, Boof has given us a compulsory day off. Even the biggest cricket obsessives in the team were ordered not to practise. No training, no work, and that goes for the support staff too.

I slept in until 8 o'clock, which is a big sleep for me. A few of the boys are tired after indulging last night, and

THE ASHES TOUR STARTS

most of us are just chilling around the hotel. A handful of the boys are going to the Formula 1 Grand Prix. I'm sure they'll have a great day, especially if Mark Webber wins. The Wallabies beat the Lions last night in the Second Test, we've won in Somerset, so let's turn this summer around!

Monday 1 July. **Worcester.**

Having given us a day off yesterday, Boof and our team manager Gavin have kept us extra busy today.

We started at 7.30 am with a novelty: an illicit drug test. Cricket Australia is bringing in hair testing for the first time, and eleven of us had to have a sizeable hunk of hair cut off and taken away. It's been explained to us that hair shows the presence of drugs in your system for far longer than urine, so it's a more accurate form of testing. It's certainly a new experience for me, but they can cut my hair any time they like.

After that I went straight into some rehab with Alex, which was necessary after a four-day match, and then a three-hour training session. Freshened up by our day off, the boys worked very hard. Darren set up different sections in separate nets to work on particular skills: one involved facing spin bowling, another had bowling machines set up with the ball swinging, and another net was for seam bowling. I think we all enjoyed working with such focus and intent.

After training came some pre-Test media commitments: some guys had an open media session, others had to do interviews for Cricket Australia TV at the hotel, and all of us had our head shots done for Sky television; these are the little cameos you see when guys walk out to bat.

There's always time for team fines, levied by a committee of Brad Haddin, James Pattinson and Peter Siddle. When I transgress, the boys have decided not to fine me as an individual. Instead, I have to pay 25 per cent of the total fines that the team pays. So they're taxing me based on the overall team performance. I guess that's the captain's lot. I didn't quite agree! But you're wasting your time arguing with that lot.

To cap off the day, Peter Brukner ran another team trivia night, a lot of laughs. This one was more of a general knowledge test, on cricket, the Ashes, music, you name it.

Tuesday 2 July. **Worcester.**

If I wanted one thing from the warm-up first-class games, it was for the batsmen to score runs. In Taunton and here today, we've got exactly that. Today was terrific – 4/340 and everyone amongst the runs.

It was overcast all day at the County Ground, allowing for a bit of movement in the air, but Shane Watson batted fantastically to make his first hundred on tour. It's great to see Watto hitting it so well again, and the certainty of knowing he's back at the top of the order seems to have worked a treat. Chris Rogers went beautifully for 75, carrying on the good form he's been showing for Middlesex. Then Eddie and I made half-centuries to round it off. Fantastic batting practice, just what we needed.

It's true that the wicket was very flat, and Worcester didn't give us their first-choice bowling attack. It'll be different in the First Test. But you know, I don't care. It's good to get confidence and time in the middle. Any bowler can get you out at any time; it's the same ball whether it's delivered by James Anderson or a young newcomer at Worcester. You can only beat the opposition you're given. And my philosophy is, you always aim to make the most of what you've got. That goes for a game, a throwdown session, or facing the best bowlers in the world in an Ashes Test. You set your standards for excellence, and aim to achieve that in every situation.

The bottom line is, we're moving through the gears towards where we want to be next week, and today was another great step in the right direction.

Wednesday 3 July. **Worcester.**

A lot of attention has been given to selecting our best top six batsmen. On the bowling side, it's also complex.

James Pattinson, Mitchell Starc, Peter Siddle and Nathan Lyon played the first tour game as the best way of managing their workload. But it's not a closed shop. There's a chance for any of the other bowlers – Jackson Bird, Ryan Harris, James Faulkner and Ashton Agar – to make a push. We want to give everyone an opportunity.

Today they gave an outstanding performance. On this flattest of flat wickets, they took seven Worcestershire wickets in a consistent day-long effort. 'Rhino' Harris, who's got a fantastic Test average and is still working his way towards full fitness, generated good pace in his first spell. Jackson Bird – who was man of the match in the last Test match he played, in Sydney in January – got four wickets and was the destroyer. And then there's the teenager Agar. I've never played with him, so this is the first time I've seen him. He's a tall, willowy left-armer with an easy action and amazing natural coordination. He's just a born athlete. I'm not surprised the selectors have fast-tracked him, and he impressed Boof in the Australia A games. He took two good wickets today and bowled quite nicely. I wouldn't be surprised if he plays a part in this Ashes series.

Thursday 4 July. **Worcester.**

The plan was clear again today and went like clockwork. If only, speaking as a captain, it always went like this!

THE ASHES TOUR STARTS

We took Worcester's last three wickets quickly, with Ryan Harris very fast and accurate. As a batting unit, we'd moved beyond just wanting to have a hit and stake a claim for Test selection. Darren and I wanted to see attacking intent and a scoring rate of four to five an over so we could declare and have 20 overs at Worcester tonight.

So it went. Phil Hughes batted brilliantly again, for a fourth time in four innings, scoring 86 runs. Steve Smith made a good 43 to go with his half-century in the first innings. And it was nice for me to have some time in the middle. Getting 124 off 98 balls is as good a medicine as anything I can get from the doctor or the physio – with all due respect!

I'm the type of player who needs some time in the middle to get my confidence going. I can't just turn up after a long break and feel self-assured straight up. Some guys can, but not me. After not batting for a couple of months, it's reassuring to know I can make a hundred, no matter who's bowling. It only takes one ball to get you out.

The fundamental sign for me that I'm batting well is my balance. The keys are being still at the crease and getting my body moving in the direction I'm hitting the ball. I don't want to be overbalancing and going across my stumps, which makes me vulnerable to an LBW. I'm at the crease thinking about staying still, then moving in the direction I'm hitting the ball. It sounds simple, doesn't it? If only!

We've got a big job ahead of us to win on this wicket, but we got the big one, Nick Compton, just before stumps. Maybe the reality of losing his Test spot is hitting him now. It's happened to me at a similar stage of my career, so I know how he's feeling.

Friday 5 July. **Nottingham.**

In the final analysis, the wicket at Worcester was too dead and flat for us. Worcestershire played quite defensively, determined on drawing, and there wasn't enough bite in the pitch for either the seamers or the spinners, Ashton Agar and Steve Smith.

Overall, I'm very happy with the four days. The players have got a lot out of it, particularly the batters. I was happy with how the bowlers tried to find different ways to get batsmen out on such a dead track. In the circumstances, taking 15 wickets was good. I'm very excited about Ashton Agar and how quickly he's improving. You can see it happening before your eyes, and as a captain that's a satisfying thing.

Boof injected a lighter note today by putting on a set of whites and a baggy green cap and running out the drinks. I told him he should stay out there. He's trying to bring some enjoyment in, alongside the hard work. He loves having a beer with the boys and makes a point of us all celebrating each other's successes. He's also as well-planned as any coach I've played under. I reckon we'll have a great partnership.

So that's it for our eight days of cricket before the Ashes. It's all been about giving every player the opportunity to push for selection in the First Test. They've got that, so now the selectors have seen all of them and have to decide which eleven to go with. The boys should be proud of how they've prepared. I think we're 99 per cent right for the Test.

We've just arrived in Nottingham, after hopping on the bus straight from the game. Tomorrow's a day off, part of a four-day program to get our minds ready, so we walk onto Trent Bridge full of belief.

Saturday 6 July. **Nottingham.**

We had a day off today, which was lovely for all the guys: a recovery day for the bowlers, who were tired after working hard on the Worcester wicket, and for me, four or five sessions with team physio Alex. I've just seen Grant Baldwin, the massage therapist, too. My back pulled up a bit stiff after batting for a few hours at Worcester, but it's been necessary to get some game time into my legs. It's not just the batting, but standing for hours in the field, crouching for every ball in slips, and all the ordinary stuff you do on the field. No matter how much rehab I have, there's no substitute for game time. At any rate, the rest and treatment will do it good.

In our team room at the hotel, we watched the deciding rugby Test between the Wallabies and the Lions. I'm sure some of the southern-states boys struggled to understand the technicalities of the rules. Unfortunately it didn't take much to work out what was going on in the game: the Wallabies were outplayed by a better team. It only adds to our motivation: we can be the team that turns the year around for Australian fans.

Having a day off offers a good chance to pause, take stock and contemplate the challenge ahead. I've spent time on my own today, getting my mind right for this First Test match. As in the last couple of years, I go through a routine of mental training against the particular opposition I'm preparing to play. I've been sitting on the couch or lying on the bed with my eyes closed, picturing the bowlers – Anderson, Broad, Finn, Swann, Bresnan – fixing an image of them running in to bowl to me. I see them on Trent Bridge, coming from the Pavilion end or the Radcliffe Road end, with the distinctive old stands in the background. I see them in sunshine and under cloud, I feel whether it's warm or cool, and I 'face' them with the ball swinging or not, spinning or not. I 'feel' my balance and 'play' positive shots.

I'm not big on meditation as such, but while I'm alone I've been listening to music to clear my mind. I don't have any special favourites: it's mainly Top 40 songs that Kyly has put on my iPod. It helps me focus on what lies ahead. All of this ticks the last box in my preparation. I'll put in a bit more of this quiet time between now and the match, so that, come Wednesday, I'm cherry-ripe.

Sunday 7 July. **Nottingham. Morning.**

Now that we're in the First Test venue, a lot of the team's partners have flown in to enjoy the game. Unlike in the old days, when partners were banned completely or had to stay in a different hotel, it's relaxing to have a bit of domestic normality. A number of the team have young children as well, and it must be a real thrill for them to see their little ones – again unlike the old days, when cricketers would miss six months of seeing their children growing up.

Anyway, last night it wasn't kids we had to worry about. I went to bed at 10.30 pm, expecting a nice full night's sleep. At about 2.45 am, the hotel was woken by a *screaming* fire alarm. The entire Park Plaza Hotel had to be evacuated. So there we were, in the main thoroughfare of Nottingham – a big multi-lane road called Maid Marian Way – the team and all the other guests, scratching our heads wondering what was going on.

It goes without saying that this was not an easy time to be getting out of bed and standing out in the cool air, but it was quite funny seeing everyone in their nightwear. There were wives and partners and children, already battling jet lag, staggering about trying to come to terms with the incident. During the 2009 tour, a similar thing happened, and we found out later that someone in the Barmy Army had set off the alarm to get under our skin. So this morning, Brad Haddin, Phillip Hughes and Peter Siddle, who were there on that tour, were saying, 'It's started all over again!'

Sunday 7 July. Nottingham. Afternoon.

In two Ashes tours and numerous other visits, I don't think I've ever experienced a hotter day in England. The sun really belted down. We were a bit tired after the interruption to our sleep, but once we got used to the heat at training it was nice, actually. It reminded us of a summer's day at home. There's always a feeling that we Australians are more comfortable in high heat than the English, so let's hope it continues.

I didn't bat or do any training aside from some slips catching at the end, as my back had felt stiff when I woke up (for the second time). As a result, I was able to spend the session watching the team.

The boys trained very hard. Their fielding was sharp, their bowling was full of energy, and the batting was focused on defence. As I've made clear all along, we need to place a very, very high price on our wickets. The flat tracks in Taunton and Worcester haven't challenged us as much as the Test matches will, and we really need to be watertight. Then, when we get set, we have to keep concentrating on every ball and get on with the job.

Speaking of pitches, I wandered out to the centre of Trent Bridge to take a look at the Test strip. It's a beautiful venue, and its reputation is that it doesn't turn very much. It does swing, though, both with the new ball and reverse with the old ball; I remember from 2005 a devastating spell of reverse swing from England's Simon Jones. From the look of it, this one will certainly provide reverse swing, and probably spin too. We were expecting dry wickets, but this one is much drier than I thought. With three days still to go, and in hot weather, unless they water it the pitch is going to have cracks in it come the start of the Test match. But at the same time, it looks like an excellent batting wicket. The rationale is that the county club that hosts the Test match has a lot riding on it, financially, and wants it to go the full five days. To me, this one looks like it will test the batsmen's patience and technique, and the bowlers' ability to maintain pressure over long spells.

I went back to the nets. The selectors, Rod Marsh and Darren Lehmann, were watching David Warner and Ed Cowan batting at the same time, side by side. It seems to be a bat-off between the two of them, a pretty tough situation because they've worked well together as opening partners for the past 18 months. It's hard for

Davey to be assessed on his net form, after being stood down from all cricket for four weeks, but it's the only indication the selectors will have.

It's very different for me, not being part of the panel. Rod and Darren watch the players themselves, and they have the NSP chairman, John Inverarity, here as well to provide a casting vote if necessary. Darren's made it clear that he's big on basing selection on performance on tour, so the players should have a good idea of where they stand. But everyone's made some runs here, and David Warner has been our opening batsman for nearly two years, so a lot of it will come down to fine judgments.

Today at practice, I had a chat with Rod and Darren about the wicket and what I believe we need to have success. They told me their views, and we debated the merits of various options. I'd say they are 95 per cent of the way towards making their decisions by the time they consult me. From here, it's up to them to pick the best eleven. They'll hand that to me, and I'll work out the batting order.

Sunday 7 July. **Nottingham. Night.**

We just got back from dinner in the hotel restaurant. There was a significant little encounter. We'd come in from our team meeting and were sitting there minding our own business when in walked Kevin Pietersen, Matt

Prior, James Anderson and Jonathan Trott. It was the first time we've had face-to-face contact with any of the England Test players, and was one of those 'moments' you always have at the start of a series. I sensed a bit of awkwardness on both sides. We'd just been talking about them in our meeting. They looked uncomfortable, walking past all of us.

It was good for me to take note of our boys' faces. I don't think anyone was intimidated, that's for sure. That first encounter is a noteworthy little part of an Ashes tour, which I find fascinating.

Monday 8 July. **Nottingham. Afternoon.**

We had another good training session, and I had a bat. All the players have now been told individually if they're in the eleven, but we're not announcing it until the toss of the coin on Wednesday. In the meantime, the players will have time to get their heads around playing in an Ashes Test match.

Darren and I are both big fans of inviting past players into the team group to talk to us about cricket and give us a sense of the great tradition we're inheriting. As Don Bradman said, we're all just custodians of this wonderful game. With that in mind, we've invited Glenn McGrath to come in on Wednesday and present the baggy green to a player making a debut.

That debutant will be Ashton Agar. I told Ashton he would be batting at number eleven. We all know he's a better batsman than that, but as a 19-year-old coming in for his First Test, I don't want to put him under any added pressure, and besides, I'd be risking being put in a headlock by asking any of the fast bowlers to bat at number eleven. I joked to Ash in the nets, 'Hey, a number eleven has never made a Test hundred. You never know!'

It's tough on Nathan Lyon, who took nine wickets in our last Test match in India. Fortunately I don't have to sit down with him and explain the decision as a selector. Instead, we had a chat where I assured him he is still an important member of the squad, and I'm sure he'll be playing a big part in this tour.

The whole England team trained after us today. During the crossover period, they sat in the same lunch room as us, at a separate long table having their meal while we had ours. Like that moment in the hotel restaurant, it's one of those signposts to the opening of the series. Two full teams, in their training gear, in the one room. It's finally happening!

There's what I would call an atmosphere of professional respect, rather than either familiarity or hostility, between the teams. I'm polite to all of the Englishmen, and will say g'day to anyone. James Anderson is the one who prefers not to talk to me. I didn't read his book, but from what I heard, he had a crack at me. That's fine. He's a fast bowler, and if I was his captain I'd want to see a bit of mongrel in him too. I doubt it's personal, though, because we don't know each other. If you have longevity in the game you must be a decent person, because if you're not, you get thrown out. I don't have any personal problems with any of the English players.

At any rate, I'm a whole lot more focused on us than I am on the English.

Monday 8 July. **Nottingham. Evening.**

Tonight we had our last team meeting before the Test match. Darren ran the meeting, and then I announced the eleven to the whole squad. For the guys involved, if they want any of their family to come over, they can then get that organised. Ashton Agar has already arranged for his parents and his two younger brothers to get on the first available flight from Melbourne.

I made it clear that aside from telling immediate family, we wanted to keep the identity of the final eleven in-house. We're not telling the media. I had a quick chat with Ashton, not saying much apart from wishing him all the best and telling him that if he keeps playing the way he has been, he can't fail.

All the guys are fully fit. We did have a little bit of a late scare with Phillip Hughes hurting his calf after training, so we'll check on that tomorrow. Meanwhile, the selectors have decided David Warner is going to fly to Africa to join an Australia A team there, to get some match practice. They want to retain the option of picking him later in the series, if necessary, so he needs time in the middle.

Tuesday 9 July. Nottingham. Evening.

Today was another beautiful sunny, warm day; I don't know what they mean when they slag off English weather! Only joking. We had an optional training session, for guys to put a finishing touch to their preparation if they want it. Everyone went except the Test fast bowlers – Pattinson, Starc and Siddle – who know they've got a hard five days ahead of them. Phillip Hughes saw the physio about his calf, but they're both happy and there's no problem.

For me, the day before a Test match is about going through a final set of routines. I went to the dressing room and set up my gear: shirts on hangers, pads on the seat, bats lined up, all the rest of my stuff organised the way I always have it. Each person has his own ways.

I have a few nerves in my system, so I had a bat today to work them out. Nothing too severe – in fact I think I'm probably a fraction less nervous than at this stage on previous tours. I've played a lot of Test cricket and am as excited as I've ever been. I just want to go out and play the way I have for the last few years.

THE ASHES TOUR STARTS

In the two pre-match press conferences, with the Australian media yesterday and the all-in today, I've been asked whether this series is the make-or-break of my captaincy. I absolutely reject that. I have three main objectives over the next 18 months: winning the Ashes here, retaining the Ashes at home, and winning the World Cup on home soil. That's the next stage in my captaincy, and that's what I'm focused on. I don't think you can judge anyone on five Test matches, which are just a slice of that overall career. I'd like to think that I won't become a 'good' or 'bad' captain based on our result here. I'm accountable for our performances and have been all along, and will be as long as I'm in the job. That goes over a long period, not just one series. Don't get me wrong – I am desperate to win this series.

To be honest, my own place in history as a captain is the last thing on my mind. I'm thinking about the coming game and our whole team. All the boys are in a really good place. We're prepared as well as we could be, and I'm proud of how the guys have conducted themselves in training and in the games. There's an excitement in the camp. It's not a scared excitement – I've seen that before – but a good excitement, a sense of eagerness for whatever challenges come our way. This is an Ashes series. I'm ready. We're ready.

It feels like the night before Christmas.

4

THE FIRST TEST MATCH

Wednesday 10 July. Nottingham.

Well, that was an interesting day to say the least: 14 wickets on what looked like a very flat and dry wicket! Probably entertaining for the crowd, but not exactly a proud day for the batsmen on both sides.

Before play, we had Glenn McGrath on the field to present Ashton Agar with his cap. Glenn made a nice speech, the theme of which was 'Never, ever give up'. It was good for all of us to hear that. The game isn't over until the last ball is bowled. Ashton himself got pretty emotional, as you'd expect, but I was also delighted to see how much pleasure all the boys took from the occasion. Almost everyone in the squad has played a Test match, so we know how Ashton feels – though none of us was 19 years old when we got our Test caps! It's great to see a young kid so excited, and he gave a shot of energy to all of us.

Kumar Dharmasena, the former Sri Lankan off-spinner who's one of our umpires this week, asked me, when he saw the line-up, how good a bowler Ashton is. I said, 'He's good, but he's an even better batsman.'

I had to assess the conditions before the toss. As at most English venues, you have to look up, not down. The pitch was dry and flat, as we knew, but a cool change had come in overnight and the sky was overcast. This usually means the ball is going to swing about early. But they've been saying that Trent Bridge doesn't produce as much swing as it used to, and we didn't know how long the cloud would stay. That, with the dryness of the wicket, suggested to me that it was still a bat-first situation.

It was academic in the end, as I called incorrectly. There's quite a funny story to the toss. Alastair Cook came out with what I think was his favourite one-pound coin. All through the tour, Chris Rogers has been claiming that English pound coins are heavier on the tails side than the heads – just a tiny bit, but enough to make a difference. I guess this is the kind of experience you get after years in county cricket! Jimmy Pattinson has been running trials with three coins, and reckons he's found proof that they come up heads more

THE FIRST TEST MATCH

often. I've been saying, 'You're dreaming!' – but when Alastair tossed the coin I called heads just in case. It fell tails-up. Alastair said he'd bat. I didn't really mind, as I thought batting would be very challenging in the first session.

The aim was to bowl full and let the ball swing. I gave Patto and Mitchell Starc six overs each at Cook and Root. Patto bowled from the Pavilion end and Starcy from the Radcliffe Road end, because there was a cross-breeze blowing that helped Patto's outswing and Mitch's inswing. There had been so much excitement in the build-up, though, that the nerves of actually being on the field were affecting everyone, batsmen and bowlers alike. The outcome was that we bowled too much on both sides of the wicket and didn't make the English openers play enough balls.

In the ninth over, it was a ball that didn't swing that gave us our first wicket. We know Cook's least favoured shot is the off drive, and we've had some success over the years pitching it full outside his off stump and getting him to play a shot he's not fully comfortable with. He's very good at waiting and frustrating you into bowling short, and he just eats up anything at waist height that he can pull or cut. We kept bowling it full, and eventually he lost the waiting game, flashing at one that kept going across him. It was great to break the ice.

Jonathan Trott looked in fine touch from the first ball. The floodlights were on it was so dark, but he seemed untroubled by the swing. I brought Ash Agar into the game in the 16th over, wanting to get him involved early to help his nerves. I set a pretty defensive field for him. His first ball to Trott was a loose full toss, and I was hoping that the batsmen would try to go after him and destroy his confidence before he got started, and play a false shot. To Ash's credit, he was the first bowler to throw Trott out of sync. There was a leading edge and a few misses, which sent Trott back into his shell a bit.

Peter Siddle had been short on wickets in the lead-up games, but he's the fifth-ranked Test bowler in the world and I know what he can do. His first spell, from the Pavilion end, was a bit inconsistent and I took him off after four overs. I switched him to the Radcliffe Road end, hoping it might suit him better. I'd like to say it was a stroke of captaincy genius, but my true feeling was just that any change might help. His first ball from that end tailed away from Root and yorked him. Sidds can be unstoppable once he gets a head of steam, and we were all around him, revving him up.

I took Sidds off after a short spell to give Starcy a bowl. We felt that he could frustrate Kevin Pietersen by bowling a fourth or fifth stump line. But Starcy wasn't at his best in that spell, and Pietersen and Trott got through to lunch.

If it had been a hot and sunny day, we'd have been happy with 2/94. But with the amount of movement

THE FIRST TEST MATCH

our bowlers were getting under the heavy cloud, I felt we could have got more wickets. The young bowlers, playing their first Ashes Test, were understandably excited, and maybe nerves had affected them. In any case, we wanted a bit more consistency now, just plugging away in the right areas and letting the ball do the work.

Watto is the ideal bowler for that job, and he brought in a measure of control. He tightened things up, and then Sidds, coming back at the Radcliffe Road end, went wide on the crease and bowled Trott – the big breakthrough, as we felt he was seeing the ball better than any of the others.

Sidds doesn't think he bowled his best today, and says he got lucky, but he really led the attack from that point. He took five wickets in the space of eight or nine overs and got us a very pleasing result in the end. Starcy and Patto chipped in with some late wickets, and we got England out for 215, which at the start of the day we would definitely have been happy to take.

There was still a fair bit going on with the ball, though, in the air and off the track. On the upside for us, Stuart Broad had taken a knock on the right shoulder or upper arm while he was batting, and the new ball was taken by Anderson and Finn. Nobody wants to see someone injured, but if England is going to be down a bowler, we'll look to exploit that. I remember how Patto's injury in Adelaide changed the course of our Test match against South Africa, and we'd like to grind England down here the way the Proteas did to us.

Watto and Chris Rogers started out with great intent. Watto cracked three boundaries in no time, and looked very happy at the top of the order, as he has all tour. Chris was compact and safe. I was hoping to settle in and watch some good batting for the rest of the afternoon when Watto went for another big drive and nicked Finn to slip.

A ball later, I was walking out there, wearing a vest in the cool weather. Ed Cowan had caught some sort of stomach bug from his young daughter Romy, and had spent a lot of the day off the field. He said he was fine to bat, but he played an out-of-character shot on the first ball and edged Finn.

The crowd was singing as I walked out, but not for me. I love how English crowds get involved, and they'd been fairly quiet through the day. Not now.

Finn's hat-trick ball was a good one, and I was lucky to miss it. Anderson was on at the other end, and looked full of energy, but his first ball I hit right out of the middle in front of square leg. Unfortunately for me, it went nowhere, hitting the close-in fieldsman instead. I felt good having got one in the sweet spot, but as usual, nervy about getting off the mark.

I felt okay for the next ten minutes or so, until Anderson bowled a very good ball that moved away late and just clipped the outside half of my off stump. Bowlers are drilled in aiming at the top of off stump, and if they can do it with some away movement, they'll get most batsmen. I suppose someone might have cover-driven that ball for four. I should have taken a bigger stride forward in defence, and then I'd have had it covered. One thing I do know, though, is that the way things are going, I'll get a second chance in this Test match.

After getting out, I watched from the balcony. Batting was tough going. Chris Rogers really impressed me, and was very unlucky to be given out LBW to a ball that you'd have to say could have missed the leg stump. In this series, Hawk-Eye only has to show part of the ball hitting the stump and, if the onfield umpire has given it out, the third umpire will confirm that decision. That's a big weight to place on an imprecise tool, but that's the way it is, and it's the same for both teams. I felt sorry for Chris though, as he was batting with great assurance, which was fantastic to see after his five years out of the team.

England bowled well in the conditions, wasting far fewer balls than we had. But Steve Smith and Phillip Hughes looked good and got us through to stumps – a small victory, but not meaningless. I'm hoping the sun comes out tomorrow, and am confident Steve and Phillip and the other guys can grind out some runs and bat for most of the day.

Thursday 11 July. **Nottingham.**

What an unbelievable day. I've never seen anything like it in over 90 Test matches, or in any other cricket. People who saw this will never forget it. Our job is to come here and win back the Ashes, but sometimes you have to step back and recognise that whatever the result, you can offer people memories that will have them falling in love with cricket for life. Today was one of those days.

The best news, when I woke up, was that the sun was out. I was very excited at the thought of the batting getting much easier on a flat wicket. Before the start of play, I talked to the boys and said this was a great opportunity to bat all day and build a big lead.

It looked so good for the first hour. Hughesy was playing the ball right under his nose. Knowing how much he loves some width outside his off stump, the English bowlers tried to cramp him by bowling at his body, but Hughesy is a better player than when they last saw him, and he handled it pretty comfortably. Steve Smith was in great nick. He'd taken on Graeme Swann yesterday, hitting him straight for six, and he used his quick footwork to get down and attack him. I thought he clearly won that battle. He came down and cover-drove a beautiful four to bring up his 50, and I thought we were on our way to a strong position.

Unfortunately, Smithy was the big wicket. He edged a drive, and it was about that time that Anderson started

THE FIRST TEST MATCH

to get the ball reversing, so the new batsmen were exposed to that. Hadds got a big spinning ball from Swann – not the type you want to get early in your innings – and our three pace bowlers, who are all good lower-order batsmen, nicked balls from Anderson that they could just as easily have played and missed.

From 4/108, we were 9/117. So in walked the 19-year-old. He just went out with no fear, backed himself and played his shots. It was a joy to watch, and the dressing room became a euphoric place. A last-wicket stand always frustrates the fielding team and gives extra joy to those in the dressing room, but this was a stand with a difference. We all knew Ash could bat, having seen him in the nets and the lead-up games, and he'd played some handy innings at number eight for Western Australia. I left him down at number eleven for two reasons. One, the three guys above him are all accomplished lower-order batsmen in their own right. Sidds scored a pair of 50s in our last Test in India, top-scoring, and made a first-class century on the Australia A tour. Starcy made 99 in India. Patto's Test average is in the 30s, and he has always impressed with his technique and application. So it's not like we have a genuine number eleven. The second reason was that I knew how nervous Ash would be and didn't want to put him under too much pressure.

Well, he was under pressure now, and yet he seemed the least nervous person in Trent Bridge. He got away with a stumping appeal early on, but the replay showed that his toe was making a shadow on the crease, and you couldn't be certain if he was on the crease or behind it. The third umpire correctly gave the batsman the benefit of the doubt.

Ash then swung and kept on swinging away, particularly on the pull shot. But he wasn't slogging either. He was playing every ball on its merits and showed good defensive skills among the flashing boundaries, dropping the dangerous balls at his feet.

That's not to forget Hughesy, who played an outstanding knock. He rotated the strike and hung in there with Ash. He deserves a lot of credit for a partnership that surpassed 151 – the world record in Test cricket for the last pair. The English obviously didn't know how good Ash was, and they looked confused for a while. At a certain point, it wasn't clear whether they were trying to keep Hughesy or Ash off strike.

At lunch, we were excited. I didn't say much to Ash, other than that I was so pleased with the way he was playing. I went to Hughesy and said, 'Back Ashton, he's a good player, you don't have to protect him from the strike.'

After the break, Ash and Hughesy batted even better. Ash played a whippy on drive off Anderson, and a clip off his toes off Broad. It was sensational batting, and Ash kept on smiling throughout it all like he was having a hit with his little brothers on the beach.

THE FIRST TEST MATCH

We got very nervous when Ash was in the 90s. We've had the running joke all week about a number eleven never making a century before. The boys were all sitting in the same seat they'd been in, not daring to move. Broad came on, after not doing much bowling at all, and decided to bowl bouncer after bouncer. This used to be not allowed against tail-enders, but to be fair, Ash had by now proved he was no typical tail-ender. Broad got one up and hit him on the arm, but Ash didn't seem bothered. The tactic was to prey on his nerves, if he had any, and try to get him playing an awkward shot against a ball rising above his head.

Then we had our hearts broken. Broad took forever to do up his shoelaces and arrange his field. Then Kevin Pietersen ambled over to have a chat. It was obvious gamesmanship – something we've all either done, or had done to us. Eventually Broad got around to bowling the ball, another short one. Ash absolutely creamed his pull shot – hit it too well, in fact, and was caught by Swann diving in at deep mid-wicket. I was watching from the doorway, and when I saw Swann jump up with the ball I had to pull back, about to explode. We were all shattered for Ash. He'd worked so hard and deserved a hundred. But as we know, it's never easy to make a Test century. I'm pretty sure Ashton Agar will get to 98 a few more times in his career, and he'll learn from this.

He came into the dressing room shrugging his shoulders, and you couldn't wipe the smile off his face.

I can remember my First Test match, and in that situation you're stoked that you've made *one* run in Test cricket. So he was definitely seeing it as 98 runs scored, not two runs missed out on.

Riding the wave of those 163 runs from Ash and Hughesy, we took plenty of energy into the field. Dharmasena and I had a chuckle about my pre-match comment that Ash was a batsman worth watching.

Taking two early wickets was great. Mitchell Starc swung the ball beautifully and Patto put it in the right areas. Starcy was a bit lucky to get Root caught down the leg side, and there was some dispute over whether Trott hit the ball before or after it went into his pads, but we accepted both, thank you! With a first-innings lead of 65 and two wickets down, we were full of confidence.

Cook and Pietersen were obviously big wickets now – the biggest. We realised that with the sun out and the wicket so dry, there wasn't a lot of assistance, so we tried from there to bowl very patiently and build up pressure. Ash got them both into a spot of bother, when Pietersen edged one that hit Brad Haddin on the leg, and Cook had another tangled up in his glove and hip. Pietersen chipped Ash in the air to mid-wicket, as we'd hoped, and I gnashed my teeth when it flew just clear of the fielder. So close!

In the field, the boys kept themselves amused by laying 'chewy bombs' for each other. A chewy bomb is when you leave some used chewing gum on the grass, and it 'goes off' when someone else walks up unsuspecting and steps in it. When it happens, everyone gets a big laugh, especially the bloke who has set the bomb. Anything that gets you through a long hot day, I suppose.

When stumps were drawn, we all came together and congratulated each other on a good day. Our spirit is strong. In about 50 overs, England got to the end of the day having scored only 78 runs, which I thought reflected a great effort by our bowlers. England is effectively 2/15. To me, the match feels even.

Tomorrow's a crucial day, not just in this Test match, but in the whole series. If we bowl England out tomorrow, we give ourselves a great opportunity to win this Test. That will surprise a few people and put us in a good position. It'll be hard to take another eight wickets on a flat track against class players. But if we keep bowling as we did today, we'll get the rewards for our hard work.

Friday 12 July. **Nottingham.**

This was the key day, a controversial day without doubt, and at the end of it I feel that we've shared the honours.

The light was smokier than yesterday, and it was a few degrees warmer. All day it felt like the crowd was getting sun-baked, and was quite sedate compared to what I'm used to in England. To us, having been in the subcontinent recently, it was almost like we were playing an Indian Test match. This was the test of how well we'd learnt our lessons from that series.

Chris Rogers took the field with a black armband, after the death of a friend.

Part of the plan against Cook and Pietersen was to dry them up. Cook is known for his patience, and Pietersen not so much, but we felt we could get the breakthrough if we frustrated both of them. We thought we could tie them down until the ball started reversing, and then attack a bit more. With Pietersen, it was a matter of taking the ball away from him, and with Cook it was to frustrate him until he came to us, reaching for balls he didn't normally want to hit.

As it turned out, they spent most of the morning trapped up each end. Sidds bowled around the wicket to Cook, and Starcy around the wicket to Pietersen. Cook was becalmed, but Pietersen took the bait. He hit four fours in the first half-hour, but we didn't mind him playing his shots and taking a risk or two.

I rotated the bowlers fairly quickly. Patto came on and beat Pietersen first up. Sidds thought Pietersen was vulnerable to the yorker, and speared in quite a few with great accuracy. We felt that we did frustrate them, and ultimately Pietersen went a bit too hard at a short one from Patto, and chopped it on.

Ashton Agar was bowling very well to Cook, using the rough outside the off stump, and I had the pleasure of

THE FIRST TEST MATCH

helping Ash take his first wicket in Test cricket. What a wicket to get – Cook, closing the face, getting a leading edge and popping the catch to slip. If one day someone asks if I can remember where I was when Ashton Agar took his First Test wicket, I can say, 'Yes, I was at slip taking the catch!'

With Bell and Bairstow in, our bowlers were starting to get the ball to reverse. Both Jimmy Pattinson and Shane Watson extracted some big movement in the air and were unlucky not to take a bunch of wickets. We lost referrals in the Decision Review System when I made a couple of errors. Patto appealed for LBW against Bairstow and our referral was turned down. Then Watto got the umpire's finger when he hit Bell in front, but England's referral overturned the decision. Both times, the ball had been veering off down the leg side, according to Hawk-Eye.

As far as our process is concerned, it's pretty straightforward. I talk to the people who have the best view, who are generally the wicketkeeper and first slip. If needed, we then go to the bowler, who's more emotionally involved and obviously thinks every ball that hits the pad is out. Within the few seconds we're allowed, we make a judgment call. Today we got two of those wrong, and lost our referrals. I take responsibility for making the final calls, but the replays showed that while we made mistakes, they were very, very close.

We got Bairstow and Prior, and took the second new ball. I thought that even though the old one was reversing, a new one might charge up the bowlers and give them some conventional swing. I'm not sure if it was the right decision, because the ball also began to come off the bat a lot harder.

We were holding up well through a hot day. The ball was beginning to shoot, Patto unsettled Broad with some short ones, Agar very nearly had Broad caught in close by Cowan and out in the deep by Hughes, and we were very confident we could have them out by stumps.

Then, on 6/297, the temperature in the game went up.

Ashton had bowled with great control all day, and was now a constant threat to Broad, who was verging on losing his patience nearly every ball. He went back to one, and cut at it. He got a big outside edge, which deflected off Brad Haddin's thigh and ballooned to me at slip. We were excited, of course, but it wasn't an appeal, it was just a celebration. A regulation wicket.

The surprise, as we gathered around Ash, was that Broad hadn't left. When we looked to the umpire, to our absolute astonishment Aleem Dar was saying not out. We looked back at Broad.

We kept appealing to Aleem, but he was saying nothing. I was that close to having the top of my head blow off, it was everything I could do to walk to first slip for the next over and take a few deep breaths. It's a crucial moment in Test cricket when these things happen, and a captain's job is to keep control of himself and of his team. We were at absolute boiling point. But the game wasn't going to stop, and we weren't allowed to refer the decision. The next ball had to be bowled.

I didn't hold it against Broad. It was ironic that his father, Chris, was the match referee who had recently banned the West Indian wicketkeeper Denesh Ramdin for cheating by claiming a catch he'd dropped. But I've played cricket for long enough to have seen this many times before, and it's not the batsman's job to walk – it's the umpire's job to give him out. That's what frustrated us: that it was a bad decision by the guy whose job it was. But to their credit, our boys held in their frustration. I said, 'Come on, let's get on with it,' but that's pretty much all I had to say.

Inevitably there's something you can laugh about in these moments, and the funny side of this was that I'd just stuffed about two full packets of chewing gum into my mouth, and while I was appealing, my cheek was bulging like a chipmunk with a mouthful of acorns. Mum always said, 'Don't speak with your mouth full!' and here I was being beamed around the world, with a gob full of chewing gum.

Anyway, there was nothing to laugh about at the time. I wish we could have stayed 'in the moment' and been able to forget the matter instantly. Peter Siddle bowled to Bell, and he defended it. I took my gum out of my mouth and threw it away. The game doesn't stop just because something's gone against you.

Next ball, Bell drove at a ball that tailed away, and got a nick. It flew very low between Hadds and me. Hadds dived to his right, but the ball went below his glove. Being such an outstanding keeper, Hadds would have expected to take it. Sidds was filthy – at the situation, not at Hadds – and it was one of those moments when a piece of freakish cricket could have changed the mood back our way again. I don't blame Hadds for one moment, as he kept going with great polish throughout a long hot day, and he had enough recriminations against himself. It was barely even a chance, that's how low and fast it went. It's always a good lesson, but it happens so often: the game doesn't stop.

This was one of those critical moments when the senior players have to show leadership. Jimmy Pattinson had a good appeal against Bell turned down, and umpire Kumar Dharmasena had to have a word to calm things down. But I felt that the boys showed remarkable restraint in the circumstances. Hadds and I decided to run fast between overs, like it was the first over of the day and we were full of spring, to gee the team up. We just had to show that we weren't going to lose our bottle. At the end of play, I personally went around to each of the bowlers and congratulated them. Whatever had happened in the last hour was something that involved the umpire and the batsman. Our part in the day was to have bowled and fielded with great patience and discipline, and I was proud of the boys.

The bowlers are very stiff and sore now. We've bowled something like 140 overs and tried everything we could think of to take wickets. The boys worked their backsides off, but didn't have a lot of luck.

Reverse swing and Swann's spin are going to be big factors in the second innings, but I think if we can restrict England's lead to somewhere between 290 and 315, we'll have a target we can chase down.

Saturday 13 July. Nottingham.

What a day – again! Another hot day, both in the weather and under our collars. Keeping cool is the constant challenge, both physically and metaphorically.

We were desperate to clean up England's last four wickets, both to limit the number of runs we would be chasing and to get the best of batting conditions on a pitch that is showing signs of wear, but still playing well enough.

The bowlers were exceedingly tired after how hard they'd worked yesterday, so the start was a bit ropy. The coaches and I talked about bowling with discipline, and they started a bit loosely. Then, a couple of overs in, Shane Watson and I moved away from each other in slips, each expecting the other to go for the ball, when Stuart Broad nicked one off James Pattinson. We've done so much slips catching practice that this was disappointing, but sometimes the ball flies into that exact centre point between you, so you each want to leave it for the other. Anyway, it was no excuse. I thought it was Watto's catch, and Watto thought it was my catch, and we were both feeling apologetic.

Fortunately, we didn't have to pay too dearly. Our pacemen finished off the England innings before lunch, and we were left with 311 to win – pretty much within the band I was looking for when we arrived at the ground today. We're good enough to get these runs, and the pitch, while difficult, is not a nightmare by any means.

As we became used to in India on these dry, abrasive pitches, scoring is easiest against the new ball. It was essential for Watto and Chris Rogers to build a firm foundation and put a high price on their wickets. After a play and miss at James Anderson's first ball, Watto played extremely well. I think it surprised some people that he went about his job patiently and methodically, when they might have expected him to go out and have a blast. It was a mature start. We expected no less from Chris, who was rock-steady again, providing a great example. They both got a few fours away early, but when things tightened up, they had the maturity to fight their way through the tough patches. Anderson tried to cramp Chris from around the wicket, but he was good enough to get through that period and won a small victory when Anderson was taken off, quite expensive, without a breakthrough.

THE FIRST TEST MATCH

Swann was brought on to bowl in the first over after lunch. As expected, he was going to wheel away from one end while Cook rotated his pace bowlers at the other. Or at least Anderson and Broad – Finn seems to have fallen out of favour for the moment.

Shane and Chris kept going, and in the dressing room we had a quiet feeling that we could do this. Swann was getting some turn, but it was slow off the deck and it wasn't jumping. The odd one was keeping low, but the dangerous ball that can pop up and off the glove or the shoulder of the bat wasn't in evidence. The slowness of the wicket meant that when Swann did drop short, he was quite hittable, and Chris and Shane both cashed in with some good pulls and cuts, and Shane put him away with one big sweep shot from outside off stump. Otherwise, the boys were watchful and looked to play straight.

As the afternoon session wore on, the ball wasn't swinging and the English fielding started to get a bit sloppy. This was what we wanted: for them to start questioning whether they were going to get a wicket. Shifts in pressure are subtle, but all-important. Of course you feel pressure as a batting team chasing a big total – 311 will be a record on this ground – but also, the longer a partnership goes on, the more that pressure shifts across towards the bowlers and fielders and their captain.

It was going perfectly until the drinks break in the middle of the day. Shane and Chris had been together for 24 overs. First ball after drinks, Broad got a bit of inswing and Shane played slightly down the wrong line. Aleem Dar gave him out – which proved he had a finger, after all! – but Watto had taken a big stride forward and felt that the ball had swung enough to be missing leg stump, so he made the decision to ask for a review. That was okay, as he and Chris were going so well together, and I would back Shane in that situation. In the end, it was super-close. According to Hawk-Eye, it was just nicking leg stump, which meant the umpire's call would stand. That meant a double loss for us: losing Shane, and losing a review.

Eddie Cowan was on a king pair. Any time that's the case, you're nervous, but he worked his way through it. Meanwhile, Chris was given out, caught behind off a big turner from Swann, but immediately reviewed it. Even though the English fielders were carrying on, we felt pretty safe. When someone like Chris reviews a caught-behind decision that quickly, you know he hasn't hit it. Sure enough, the ball might have made a noise when it grazed his pad, but it was nowhere near his bat.

Ed and Chris worked well together for an hour. Now it looked like this could be the big partnership we needed to build our innings around. Finn came on, but Ed hit him and Swann for some nice boundaries. Chris brought up his First Test 50, and we were all very pleased for him. It's been a long time coming, to say the least!

They got close to tea. When the tension is so high, and the batsmen are locked inside their bubble of concentration, an interval is often the last thing they need. Replacing Finn after three overs, Cook brought Joe Root on to bowl a couple of overs of what looked like some pretty regulation off-spin. Chris dealt with his first over easily, but then, on the third-last ball before the break, which Root gave a bit of air, Ed edged his off-drive to first slip.

Never a good waiter, I was eager to get out there. Chris and I were on the edge of the boundary five minutes before the umpires and the Englishmen came out to take the field. I was happy to make a statement of intent. I was very nervous, it goes without saying, but this was the type of situation I train for and live for. We needed exactly 200 to win.

Root had to bowl two balls to finish his over, and I was lucky enough to get one on my pads to turn away and get off the mark. No matter what the situation, getting that first run takes the edge off my nerves.

Cook went straight to Anderson and Broad, which was what I'd expected. Broad's first ball to me was a long hop outside off stump, but I was still a bit rusty and chopped it down past my stumps.

Chris and I set about building a partnership. It was very hot and muggy, with a feeling of rain in the air, but the clouds weren't coming in our direction. When Anderson came on, he covered the ball and bowled reverse swing both ways, which is something not many bowlers can do. I had a good sighting of how much the ball was doing. In that over, though, I played a couple of very positive forward defensive strokes, which can give me as much confidence as hitting a four. More, sometimes – I'd rather play a solid forward defence to mid-off than nick a four through second slip!

With the ball keeping low and getting soft, and the heat, it still felt like we were back in India. Broad got one past me that kept a bit low. I told myself to keep watching the ball and playing straight. The one that was on the stumps and kept low was the one to look out for.

After a nervous first 15 minutes, I called for some new gloves. My inners were soaked through. But I could feel my confidence rising. We have placed so much emphasis on defensive batting, and my balance was good as I kept out the dangerous balls. Broad slipped down the leg side a couple of times and I wasn't quick enough to get my bat on them, but leg byes were as good as runs. I then hit a solid on drive, again to the fieldsman, but in such a way that I got the sense I was going to have a good day.

In the 43rd over, after I'd been with Chris for half an hour, Anderson hit him on the body. Two balls later, Anderson got him. He bowled one with a scrambled seam, and Chris chipped the ball to mid-wicket.

It was a blow, but I have full confidence in the rest of our batsmen. Steve Smith and Phil Hughes batted positively in the first innings and were seeing the ball well. Steve is a fidgety partner, but I don't mind that. My nervous energy is always high early in my innings, and being with a guy who's on a similar wavelength doesn't bother me.

The runs weren't coming easily, though. Broad gave me one on my thigh that I was able to turn away fine for a boundary. Against Anderson, Smithy chased some wide full outswingers and hit them beautifully. The English fielders oohed and aahed, but I told Steve to keep watching the ball and backing himself.

Swann came on for Broad, and while I was getting ready to face him he stopped the play to move his fieldsmen around in a painstaking kind of way. This is often just a ploy to disrupt your concentration and make you play at the other team's tempo. My response is to think, 'No, you're going to play at *my* tempo.' So when he was finally ready, I stepped off to the side of the wicket to take off my helmet and wipe the sweat off my forehead and out of my eyes. It actually was pretty tropical. I never thought Nottingham could feel like Sydney in summer!

With the slowness of the wicket, it was hard forcing the pace against either the seamers or the spinners. The bounce and spin were varying and they were drying us up, waiting for us to play a false shot. I'd been keeping Swann out for a few overs when he bowled a looping full toss, knee-high, outside my off stump. I swung at it too hard and under-edged it towards mid-wicket.

It was difficult to find any rhythm. I played some off drives against Anderson and then Finn, but both squirted away behind point – safely, but not where I'd wanted. Patience, patience.

We got to the halfway point in the chase, 3/156, a little milestone. Then Broad came on from the Radcliffe Road end to replace Finn. He bowled me a fullish ball that wobbled a bit outside my off stump and went through a touch low. I played forward, and thought I felt my bat brush my pad on the way through. The English went up in a huge, excited appeal, but I wasn't worried. First, I wasn't sure if it had carried to Matt Prior, and second, I didn't think I'd hit it.

The umpires conferred on the carry – a worrying sign, because if I hadn't hit it the carry wouldn't matter. They referred it to the third umpire, and we waited. I spoke to Smithy, who said he hadn't seen or heard a nick.

While we waited, Kevin Pietersen challenged me. 'I thought you were a walker.' I turned around and said, 'I'm not walking because I didn't think I hit it.'

I still wasn't worried, even when third umpire Marais Erasmus sent down the message that it had carried to Prior, and Aleem Dar gave me out. I immediately referred it for the edge. We watched on the big screen, and I felt good – there was no white mark on my edge on Hot Spot. But the English had got a message from their dressing room, and they were beginning to jump about and celebrate. Soon enough, the third umpire upheld Dar's decision, and I was off. Pietersen sent me on my way with some choice words.

THE FIRST TEST MATCH

Back in the dressing room, the television showed there was the finest of marks against my edge. The third umpire has a monitor that is very high-definition, much more than the big screen we watch on the field, so that explained why we hadn't seen it from the middle. Nothing I could do about it now anyway – I was out.

People were going to compare my action with Broad's the day before, I knew that. There would be the usual declarations that 'you always know if you've hit it'. That's not true – not in my years of playing cricket, anyway. Sometimes the nick can be so fine that I haven't felt or heard it, or it's been my bat handle clicking as I played the shot. Sometimes my bat has touched my pad, or boot, or the ground. Sometimes I haven't been sure if I've jammed the ball into the ground or it's bounced before I've hit it. Sometimes I haven't been sure if the ball has hit my bat before my pad, pad before the bat, or a whole jumble. There are literally hundreds of situations where you don't know for sure. And in a Test match, under the highest pressure, you're not thinking or perceiving as clearly as you are during a relaxing hit in the backyard. My point is, there's a lot of uncertainty, and the reason we need umpires is not just because players don't want to be honest, but because they *don't know*. That was me today. I wasn't certain, so I asked for the review.

The upshot was that I was in the pavilion now, with no turning back. Nothing I could do about it now. I'm pretty good at putting these things behind me, but it was a challenge after the previous few days.

At any rate, I had to stay cool for the boys' sake. Smithy was LBW to Swann the next ball; luckily it seemed definitive, so we hadn't paid a price straight away for my using our last unsuccessful review.

Neither Hadds nor Hughesy had faced a ball, but they were both out there, starting from scratch. A few minutes later, the rub of the green went against us in a different way. This time, Swann bowled around the wicket to Phillip, spun one savagely, and hit him on the pads. The English appealed excitedly, but Kumar Dharmasena gave him not out, indicating that the ball pitched outside leg stump. That was certainly the way it appeared to me: the ball had turned a great deal, and was going to hit middle. That and the television replay suggested it had pitched outside leg.

But this time, the third umpire overruled the onfield umpire. The only common denominator was that it was another decision in England's favour. When the wicket-to-wicket blue strip was laid on the TV replay, it showed the ball pitching right on the outside line of leg stump. Not much we could say about that. Our eyes had deceived us.

I moved Ashton Agar up to number eight, which he'd certainly earnt with his first innings. He and Hadds had some nervous moments in the last half-hour, but got through Anderson's return for the last three overs, and brought us to stumps at 6/174. Before going off, Hadds found Ian Bell to shake his hand and congratulate him on his century, which is typical of our vice-captain.

After play, I did something a bit unconventional. Normally, the captain's press conference is after the end of the match. Each day before then, the media manager brings out one outstanding performer, or the coach, to talk about each day. It's not expected that the captain will talk to the media during the match. But I knew there would be a lot of debate about my dismissal, and I wanted to nip it in the bud. I told our media officer Matt Cenin that I would be happy to be the chosen player to talk about the day. In interviews, I repeated that I had thought I'd missed the ball, but accepted that I'd hit it. I wasn't prepared to enter into any discussion about the merits or otherwise of the system. I've got enough to think about. But the bottom line is, it's the same for England and us, we all know the rules, and they apply equally.

When the boys were in the dressing room, I told them we had to believe we could win. This Test match has been a rollercoaster, and we are due for some ups. After our first innings, we know anything is possible. Six wickets down is probably two more than I'd have liked to be at this stage, but Hadds is just the guy for this situation, having made lots of runs against England in the past, and we're all aware of what Ashton can do. Starcy, Sidds and Patto are all genuine number eight or nines who have made good runs in Test matches. We don't have any bunnies. The pitch is playing well enough for a fourth and fifth day. We just have to believe.

Sunday 14 July. **Nottingham.**

Test cricket's a great game. I don't say that to be flippant: it really is. We have just played in one of the best matches of all time. People will talk about it for years. One day, we'll talk about it in that way too. But for now, as captain of this team, it hurts too much to be philosophical. I feel wrung out.

So much happened over the five days of this match, but there was a full Test's worth of action in the two and a half hours that were played today.

I was a spectator, like most people. My emotions stayed fairly level, because I was confident from the start that we could win, and as I felt the excitement rise as the other boys began to believe it.

The plan for Hadds and Ash was not to hurry or panic. The pitch was playing well enough as long as you didn't lose patience. A lot of balls were hitting the inside half of the bat, so they had to play straight. Guys like Brad and Ashton, who like to get on with the game, will get too impatient if they just block for over after over, so they also had to hit the ball hard when it was there to

My embroidered blazer and pouch. The '43' signifies that I'm the 43rd Australian Test captain. The '389' signifies that I'm the 389th person selected to play Test cricket for Australia.

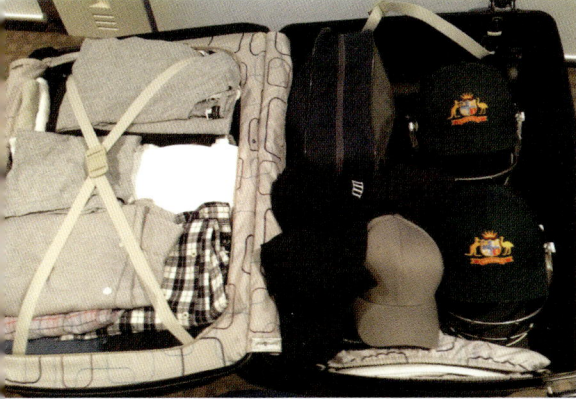

My suitcase, with Australian batting helmets.

Pouch, cap and personal messages.

David Warner's suspension started the day of this press conference, which he and I held in London. We also had a private chat about his future. It was a low moment, but it was the beginning of his road back into the team.

The replacement of Mickey Arthur as coach was the last thing I expected 18 days from the First Test. In his press conference at Bristol, he was struggling with more than one personal crisis.

GEOFF CADDICK/AFP/GETTY IMAGES

Shell-shocked. Darren Lehmann and I hold a press conference in Bristol after Mickey Arthur's removal as coach. My main concern is the effect it will have on the team 18 days before the Ashes series starts.

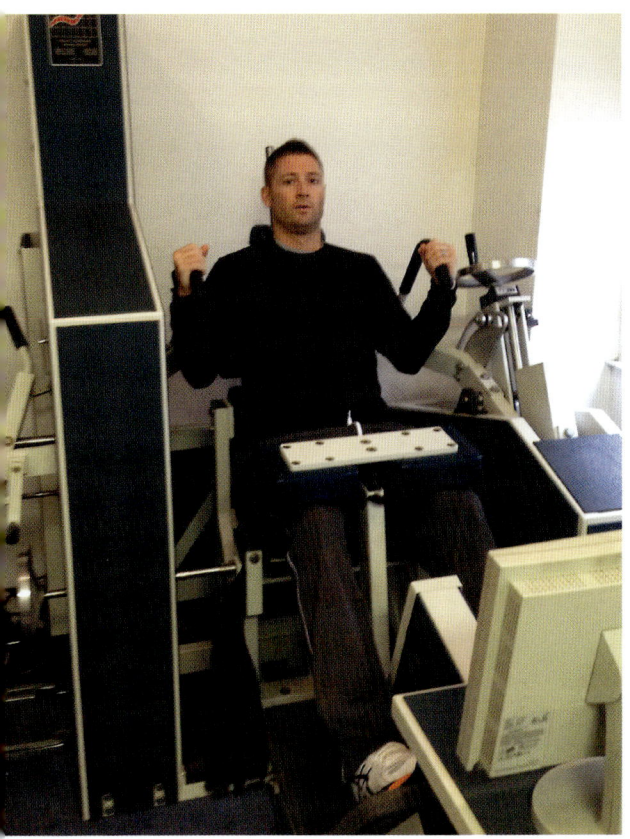

On the MedX machine working on my back. It was to be near this machine in London that I had to leave the Champions Trophy squad.

The first team trivia night, compered by Dr Peter Brukner (in black hat and red striped blazer). A lot of head-scratching going on. In the foreground with beard is my partner in the quiz, Phillip Hughes.

With a full rack of Spartan bats sent to England. I actually go through them all and sample them for feel before choosing which to use.

A night out in Nottingham. At about 2.45 am, three mornings before the First Test match, a fire alarm had all the squad and support staff out of their hotel beds and on Maid Marian Way.

Me out at dinner with Kyly, who travelled with me throughout the Ashes tour.

With Hugh Jackman, a great supporter of the Australian team and self-confessed cricket tragic, in the changing room at Lord's. A week later, Kyly and I went to see Hugh's new movie, *The Wolverine*, in Brighton.

As new head coach, Darren Lehmann added his experience, cricket knowledge and love of life to the team.

At dinner in London to celebrate the birthday of Suzanne Goodwin, wife of Geoff, the Australian team's long-time bus driver in England. From left: Me, Kyly, Suzanne. On right side of table, from front to rear: Brad Haddin, fielding coach Steve Rixon, Shane Watson. Also, up the back are Geoff, Ryan Harris, media officer Matt Cenin, Shane's wife Leigh Furlong and team manager Gavin Dover.

The closest I will get to the Ashes: Alastair Cook and I pose with the urn at Trent Bridge, Nottingham, before the First Test match.

The first day of the First Test match feels like Christmas: all excitement and anticipation. Our faces, and those of the Englishmen, indicate the nerves that will affect both sides' play on day one.

In the huddle: I'm stressing discipline, bowling to our plans, positive intent, and working for one another.

Late in the day, I get a good ball from James Anderson.

I told umpire Dharmasena to watch out for Ashton Agar's batting. The whole world was watching it when he made a world record for a number eleven on debut on day two at Trent Bridge. For his effort, he won our coach's man of the match blazer.

Trent Bridge is one of the prettiest and most historic grounds in England. On day three, I'm leading the boys out, thinking about how much work we have in front of us.

know where I was when Ashton Agar took his first Test wicket: catching Alastair Cook at first slip. Day three at Trent Bridge.

Stuart Broad played a valuable second innings for England. As he sweeps Ashton Agar, I'm trying to anticipate an edge.

The big moment on day three, when Aleem Dar gives Broad not out. I have to concentrate on keeping the boys' frustration in check: which I hope to achieve, despite a mouthful of chewing gum!

The heartbreaker. With 14 runs separating the teams, Cook calls for a referral after Brad Haddin edges Anderson, Trent Bridge day five. I asked Hadds if he hit it, and he said yes.

At the Australian High Commission in London, I surprise the boys by giving them character appraisals before an audience of dignitaries. Watto's thinking, yes, one day he might be in The Rolling Stones.

Her Majesty Queen Elizabeth II is gracious and businesslike as she meets the team ahead of the first day of the Second Test at Lord's Cricket Ground. She's not the first or last person in the world to take a shine to 'Rhino' Harris.

Rhino steaming in at Lord's, where he makes an immediate impact on day one. He'll end the tour as our man of the series.

Brad Haddin broke our tour selector Rod Marsh's 30-year-old world record for dismissals in a series. Here is one of his best, catching Matt Prior off Steve Smith, day one at Lord's.

On a long third day at Lord's, wickets are few and far between. We're appealing, but something in our body language suggests we're not too confident.

It's great to see Usman make his half-century. But the job's not done yet, and soon we would both be out.

THE FIRST TEST MATCH

be hit. It's a fine line. But at least there was no problem with time: all day to score 137 runs.

The weather had cooled down, but it was still sunny, after an early mist had burned off. Cook started with Swann and Anderson, and they bowled tightly. Hadds normally bats well out of his crease, so Prior stood up to the stumps for Anderson to keep him in check. Hadds got the first runs of the day when he late-cut Anderson, fine of gully.

After his freewheeling first innings, Ash showed that he has more than one game. He steadily kept Swann out before lapping a nice fine sweep for two. The Englishmen continued to slow the game down, calling a groundsman on to thump down the ground while Ash waited for Swann to start an over, but Ash has an old head on his 19-year-old shoulders, and responded with a lovely late cut.

Hadds bases his game on a solid defence, before he can be more expansive and show his superb attacking style. After a lot of blocking, he took a big swipe at Swann and hit a four, and then tried to be positive against Broad when he came on. Meanwhile, after Ash jammed a four through slips, Cook put a third man on the boundary, a sign that he was getting concerned about leaking runs. There were a few moments of panic – Ash went for a second run on a bye, and could have been run out by a direct hit from the fielder, and Hadds had our hearts in our mouths whenever he went over the field – but then

Ash cut a beautiful four off Broad, and we were getting close to bringing the target down to 100.

Anderson was bowling unchanged from the Radcliffe Road end, and just on the hour he bowled a very good ball that nipped away from Ash. Only a batsman seeing the ball well would have touched it, and the edge went to Cook at a wide first slip. These things really drive you spare. There was nothing to say that edge should have gone to the keeper or slip or right between them, as the one from Bell had done on day three. Anyway, Cook grabbed the chance.

Since the first day this has been a hard wicket for new batsmen, no matter where in the order they play, on both teams. Mitchell Starc had had a long bat in the nets this morning, and I put him above Sidds because England had surprisingly taken the second new ball. I thought that Mitchell, being a very fluent attacking batsman, might be able to score runs quickly and change the direction of the game. But Anderson was again too good — amazing stamina, too, with all the bowling he was asked to do — and Cook took another catch.

We were down, but as 'Pigeon' (Glenn McGrath) said the other day, the Australian team's theme is never to give up. Sidds batted with freedom and generally middled the ball. I was waiting for some luck to go our way, and it did when he nicked Anderson to Cook's left. It went faster than the earlier catches, and Cook put it down. But then Anderson again got one to

THE FIRST TEST MATCH

move away from Sidds, and Cook took an outstanding catch leaping to his right. Damn! They'd dropped two catches in the entire match (Swann had put down Mitchell Starc on day two), but they had cost fewer than ten runs.

From such a promising start, we'd lost those three wickets in half an hour. Anderson bowled 13 straight overs to take three wickets for 29. Finn replaced him, and Hadds found him very much to his liking. I was still surprised that England had taken the second new ball, to be honest. We needed 80 to win when Patto went in, a lot for a last-wicket pair, but only half of what the last-wicket pair had scored in our first innings. And again, Patto is not a genuine number eleven.

In a very short period, they got the target down to 40. Hadds took Finn for three straight fours over wide mid-on, and then Patto hit Finn for four and hoicked a six off Swann.

Broad came back for Finn, and slowed things down. I was wearing a path in the dressing room floor, pacing to and fro and spinning a rolled-up ball of tape in my hands. There was the odd anxious moment with the running between wickets, and a play and a miss here and there, but our boys were getting closer.

The umpires delayed the lunch break by half an hour, but it was never going to be long enough for Hadds and Patto to finish it off before the break. That was another test of their concentration. When we had

26 to win, Hadds went after Swann and lifted him over square leg. It was never going to clear the boundary, but was it going to get past Finn, who was running around? Sometimes bad luck follows you, and Finn, just taken out of the attack, put down a pretty gutsy diving attempt.

We were cheering like madmen. The ball went for four – 22 to win!

The crowd, which normally loved to sing, was too tense to make a noise. The dressing room was similar. We had a bit of a groan just before lunch when Broad stopped to tie his lace, and then to remove his entire shoe, orthotic insert and all, in a ploy to make his over the last one before the break.

We still needed 20 to win, and couldn't get them before lunch. England only needed one ball to win. So why were they the ones who wanted to get into the dressing room? The momentum was clearly with us.

Lunch came, and all I could say to Hadds and Patto was to keep going the way they were. In that situation, when batsmen are in the zone, you don't want to interrupt them or show your own nerves. Most players agree that it's easier to be out in the middle than watching from the rooms, so we tried to stay as cool and calm as possible and let them go about their own routines.

The break seemed to last forever, though. When they finally went back out there, Anderson was back on, of course. Patto chopped down his second ball, nearly onto his stumps. We all gasped. Maybe this was the rub of the green we'd been waiting for.

In Anderson's next over, Hadds played forward and kind of quit on the shot as it went past the inside edge. Or had it? The English didn't really appeal all that enthusiastically, certainly not in the same way they had been. Anderson delayed his shout, and Prior, who caught it, was restrained. But Cook, with referrals up his sleeve, sent it up to the third umpire and the rest is history.

In the dressing room, we were stunned. Again, the technology wasn't conclusive. There was a suggestion of a noise, and some sign of 'heat' on Hadds' edge, but neither showed up in the expected manner, at the same instant as the ball passed through. But the very worst thing I can do as captain is to stew over that. It's over. It was a great match. We lost.

I felt devastated for Hadds. I've played with him for a long time and I love having him on the field and in the dressing room again. I really thought today the cricket gods were going to smile on him. He's had such a hard 18 months or so, with his daughter's sickness and then being out of the Australian team. With him fighting his way back in, I thought his redemption was going to be hitting the winning runs. The first thing I asked him when he came in was, 'Did you hit it?' And he said yes, he had.

As disappointed as we are, there are so many positives to take out of this game. We had a couple of beers in the dressing room and Darren and I spoke, complimenting the boys on the fight they had shown. We are disappointed not to get over the line, but we can't let that get us down. We played well, and showed England we're here for a fight.

In a team ritual, two players are presented with coloured blazers that they have to wear all night. Boof awarded the cream blazer for man of the match to a very proud Ashton Agar. And the pink blazer, for the person in the entire group who best embodies the culture of 'one-percenters' – doing lots of little things that help everyone – is being worn by an equally deserving Nathan Lyon, who has shown himself a great team man despite the disappointment of missing a place in the eleven.

Wally Edwards, our chairman, brought the former prime minister John Howard into the rooms. John is here for the first two Test matches, and it was good to have a catch-up. I also felt it was good to introduce him to the younger players, for them to see that he's following and supporting us.

After a couple of hours at Trent Bridge, we came back to the hotel for a shower and a change, before heading out to a pub. Almost all the team came, plus support staff. From there we came back to the hotel for a players-only team dinner. The wives and partners had their own dinner at the far end of the hotel restaurant, and it was great to see them having a laugh and a good time together.

THE FIRST TEST MATCH

We can hold our heads high. We came to England being called the worst Australian team ever. I don't think anyone's saying that now. Winning respect is just the first step. We've done that.

Winning Test matches is the next.

First Test
10 July 2013. **Trent Bridge, Nottingham.**

England (first innings)

Batting		R	B	4	6	SR
AN Cook	c: Haddin b: Pattinson	13	26	2	0	50.00
JE Root	b: Siddle	30	64	6	0	46.88
IJL Trott	b: Siddle	48	80	9	0	60.00
KP Pietersen	c: Clarke b: Siddle	14	23	3	0	60.87
IR Bell	c: Watson b: Siddle	25	63	6	0	39.68
JM Bairstow	b: Starc	37	51	7	0	72.55
MJ Prior	c: Hughes b: Siddle	1	7	0	0	14.29
SCJ Broad	c&b: Pattinson	24	30	5	0	80.00
GP Swann	c: Hughes b: Pattinson	1	5	0	0	20.00
ST Finn	c: Haddin b: Starc	0	1	0	0	0.00
JM Anderson	not out	1	6	0	0	16.67
	Extras (5lb, 8w, 2nb, 6b)	21				
	Total 10 Wkts, 59.0 Overs	215			3.64 Runs/Over	

Bowling	O	M	R	W	Econ	SR	Extras
JL Pattinson	17.0	2	69	3	4.06	34.0	(2w, 1nb)
MA Starc	17.0	5	54	2	3.18	51.0	
PM Siddle	14.0	4	50	5	3.57	16.8	(1w, 1nb)
AC Agar	7.0	1	24	0	3.43		
SR Watson	4.0	2	7	0	1.75		(1w)

Australia (first innings)

Batting		R	B	4	6	SR
SR Watson	c: Root b: Finn	13	14	3	0	92.86
CJL Rogers	lbw: Anderson	16	37	2	0	43.24
EJM Cowan	c: Swann b: Finn	0	1	0	0	0.00
MJ Clarke	b: Anderson	0	6	0	0	0.00
SPD Smith	c: Prior b: Anderson	53	79	7	1	67.09
PJ Hughes	not out	81	131	9	0	61.83
BJ Haddin	b: Swann	1	2	0	0	50.00
PM Siddle	c: Prior b: Anderson	1	5	0	0	20.00
MA Starc	c: Prior b: Anderson	0	5	0	0	0.00
JL Pattinson	lbw: Swann	2	8	0	0	25.00
AC Agar	c: Swann b: Broad	98	101	12	2	97.03
	Extras (15lb, 0w, 0nb, 0b)	15				
	Total 10 Wkts, 64.5 Overs	280			4.32 Runs/Over	

Bowling	O	M	R	W	Econ	SR	Extras
JM Anderson	24.0	2	85	5	3.54	28.8	
ST Finn	15.0	0	80	2	5.33	45.0	
GP Swann	19.0	4	60	2	3.16	57.0	
SCJ Broad	6.5	0	40	1	5.85	41.0	

England (second innings)

Batting		R	B	4	6	SR
AN Cook	c: Clarke b: Agar	50	165	6	0	30.30
JE Root	c: Haddin b: Starc	5	31	1	0	16.13
IJL Trott	lbw: Starc	0	1	0	0	0.00
KP Pietersen	b: Pattinson	64	150	12	0	42.67
IR Bell	c: Haddin b: Starc	109	267	15	0	40.82
JM Bairstow	c: Haddin b: Agar	15	62	0	0	24.19
MJ Prior	c: Cowan b: Siddle	31	42	6	0	73.81
SCJ Broad	c: Haddin b: Pattinson	65	148	7	0	43.92
GP Swann	c: Clarke b: Siddle	9	28	1	0	32.14
ST Finn	not out	2	8	0	0	25.00
JM Anderson	c: Hughes b: Siddle	0	2	0	0	0.00
Extras	(13lb, 1w, 9nb, 2b)	25				
Total	10 Wkts, 149.5 Overs	375		2.50 Runs/Over		

Bowling	O	M	R	W	Econ	SR	Extras
JL Pattinson	34.0	8	101	2	2.97	102.0	(1nb)
MA Starc	32.0	7	81	3	2.53	64.0	(1w, 1nb)
AC Agar	35.0	9	82	2	2.34	105.0	(1nb)
PM Siddle	33.5	12	85	3	2.51	67.7	(2nb)
SR Watson	15.0	11	11	0	0.73		

Australia (second innings)

Batting		R	B	4	6	SR
SR Watson	lbw: Broad	46	74	8	0	62.16
CJL Rogers	c: Bell b: Anderson	52	121	8	0	42.98
EJM Cowan	c: Trott b: Root	14	43	3	0	32.56
MJ Clarke	c: Prior b: Broad	23	70	2	0	32.86
SPD Smith	lbw: Swann	17	48	2	0	35.42
PJ Hughes	lbw: Swann	0	8	0	0	0.00
BJ Haddin	c: Prior b: Anderson	71	147	9	0	48.30
AC Agar	c: Cook b: Anderson	14	71	2	0	19.72
MA Starc	c: Cook b: Anderson	1	5	0	0	20.00
PM Siddle	c: Cook b: Anderson	11	22	2	0	50.00
JL Pattinson	not out	25	57	2	1	43.86
Extras	(10lb, 0w, 1nb, 11b)	22				
Total	10 Wkts, 110.5 Overs	296		2.67 Runs/Over		

Bowling	O	M	R	W	Econ	SR	Extras
JM Anderson	31.5	11	73	5	2.29	38.2	
SCJ Broad	23.0	7	54	2	2.35	69.0	(1nb)
GP Swann	44.0	10	105	2	2.39	132.0	
ST Finn	10.0	3	37	0	3.70		
JE Root	2.0	0	6	1	3.00	12.0	

5

THE SECOND TEST MATCH

Monday 15 July. Nottingham to London.

After the wild ride of the First Test, we have three days to recover and get ourselves up again. Today was a quiet one, allowing us to switch off a little. The team bus left Nottingham at 10 am, paused for a feed at a services stop along the way, and arrived in London around 2.30 pm. We checked into the Royal Garden Hotel in Kensington, which has been the Australian team's London base for as long as I've been in the group. It's great to feel familiar with the staff, the restaurants, the surrounds, and Kensington Gardens next door. Having somewhere so comfortable just takes a lot of unknowns and distractions out of the equation. Kyly and I went out for dinner to a Chinese restaurant with some friends visiting from Australia, and had an early night.

Now to re-focus.

Tuesday 16 July. London.

For the media, the story of Mickey Arthur's sacking has become the gift that just keeps giving.

The day started routinely. I spent a session on the MedX machine, just a precautionary matter of flexing and extending my back and getting some use out of the machine while I have it nearby. I followed that with some physio with Alex, then trained with the team until 1.00 pm. We knuckled down and concentrated on our attitude, not treating it as just another practice session, but a really important part of our preparation for the Lord's Test match.

Everyone trained except Brad Haddin, who's been hit by the virus Ed Cowan had picked up after his daughter got it from a childcare centre. A few of the guys have been a bit croaky and below par, but Hadds is the only one who can't train.

I took a look at the wicket, which seems very good, with more pace and bounce than Trent Bridge. I'm expecting them to give it another mow. We're hoping they'll leave the grass on it, but don't think they will. I'm not sure yet what the selectors are thinking, but it's been

THE SECOND TEST MATCH

widely remarked that Ed Cowan and Mitchell Starc are under pressure after Nottingham.

A drug test after training was, I thought, going to be my last cricket commitment of the day, but then I was summoned to a meeting with Pat Howard, our high performance manager. He updated me on developments in Australia, where Mickey Arthur has commenced legal action suing Cricket Australia for unfair dismissal. I don't really want to think about that. As far as my Ashes tour is concerned, Darren Lehmann is now our coach and I'm thinking about this week's Test match, not what happened a few weeks ago.

But I'm getting dragged in. Pat explained that some details of Mickey's legal statement have been made public. Most damaging, as far as the team is concerned, is Mickey's allegation that my relationship with Shane Watson has been terrible, and that Mickey felt like he was the 'meat in the sandwich' between us.

As I've said until I'm blue in the face, Shane and I get on fine, even if we don't always see eye to eye. That is healthy and natural. I am frustrated about this continually being brought up. The important thing is that our relationship has improved out of sight. We know each other extremely well. The main point is that we're getting on better now than we have for a long time, so I feel that what Mickey's statement has talked about is old news and no longer relevant. People think they know what goes on in a team environment, but very few actually do. Shane and I know, so that's all that counts.

Darren's arrival as coach has been great for Shane as they have a strong mutual respect. I grabbed them together after I met with Pat and asked if Shane was okay. He said he was going great, and wouldn't be distracted by this. It seems that *we've* dealt with it, but the outside world is just catching up.

So I had to do a doorstop with media, getting the message across that this is old news and will not affect the team; the team's in a great place, and I don't want them to be distracted. I'm frustrated that I have press conferences where I'm answering all these questions when we have a Test match starting tomorrow. I can guarantee that this will not affect the boys.

But I have to bite my tongue in this job, sometimes to my own detriment. I could say some things about this whole affair that would make me look better, but that would only give the story oxygen. So instead, I do everything I can to pour cold water over it. If I cop some stick as a result, as I have before, then that's the price I pay on the team's behalf.

In private, though, I'm filthy. I had a long talk with Kyly about it tonight, pouring out my frustrations. I've supported Mickey through thick and thin, and it pisses me off that this has come up now. I sent him a text to tell him as much. He'd said that he didn't want it to come out publicly, but somehow it leaked out anyway. If

THE SECOND TEST MATCH

Mickey didn't know this was going to happen, he's been naive. I still can't believe he would allow this to happen to the team members, who had no part in his dismissal.

Afterwards, the whole team went to the Australian High Commission in London for a function with plenty of VIPs. I wanted everyone to have some fun so I thought I would take the mickey out of some of the boys.

Brad Haddin, who wasn't there because he had the flu, copped it first. I said he wasn't there because 'he is still hung-over from the other night, drowning his sorrows after losing the First Test match.' I revealed that he was 'a proud redhead and the chairman of the team's finance committee. He loves nothing more than taking money off his fellow teammates.'

Here's a digest of the others:

Chris Rogers – 'Chris is our team nerd. He enjoys long walks on the beach, coffee, movies and dancing, but all on his own.'
Shane Watson – 'We call Shane "Mr Guitar Hero" because every time you are walking down the corridors to your hotel room, he's always on his guitar. One thing you don't know about Shane is that today he is a cricketer, but tomorrow he could be in The Rolling Stones.'
Ed Cowan – 'Mr Eduardo Cowan is certainly one of a kind, to say the least. He enjoys picnics in the park. With his male friends.'

Steven Smith – 'Steven thinks he is one of the good-looking roosters in our team. He has an itch with his left hand.' (This was a reference to Steve's mannerism, which you can see if you watch him closely, of twitching his left hand upwards after he's bowled, or when he's batting, or in the field. Some of the boys enjoy taking the mickey out of it.)

Peter Siddle – 'He is the Vegan of our team whose favourite meal is soft-shell crab . . .' At this point, Sidds tried to wrestle the microphone off me, no doubt to spill a bit of dirt on the captain. I cried out, 'No! This is my time!' But Sidds explained that the soft shell reference was after he ordered a mushroom sushi roll and took a bite, only to find it was crab.

Mitchell Starc – 'Big, tall, left-armer Mitchell Starc, strong young lad. His girlfriend Alyssa Healy, who we like to call his wife, is an Australian wicketkeeper. We all believe Mitchell learnt his left-arm inswinger from Alyssa in the backyard at home.'

James Pattinson – 'If James could take one thing to a deserted island, it would be his mirror.'

Ryan Harris – 'Ryan is the scaredy-cat of our team: a big, strong, fast bowler who is petrified of heights.'

Jackson Bird – 'There's already been a song about Jackson and it goes (Here I sang, badly) *Bird, bird, bird is the word.* Jackson Bird also has a foot phobia.' Which he actually does have!

James Faulkner – 'We call James "Mr Hussey Junior". The reason is he loves getting not-outs when he bats, and his favourite colour is also red.'
Nathan Lyon – 'He is in love with Brad Haddin and was a state netball champion in school.' It may seem unbelievable, but yes, it's true that Nathan was a state netballer.
Matthew Wade, David Warner, Phillip Hughes, Usman Khawaja – 'They are our team band, One Direction.'
Ashton Agar – 'And our last player, what can I say about him? The man of the hour, Ashton Agar, is great at everything. And if any of you have some spare time tonight he will be more than happy to tell you just how good he and his brothers are at everything.'

It was a relief to defuse the tension, but now I have to put a new hat on: as a batsman. In the next 36 hours, I have to make sure I'm ready to score runs at Lord's. That's my job. I won't let anything stand in the way of my preparation.

Wednesday 17 July. London.

Today was an absolute stinker, hot and humid like Brisbane in mid-summer. We had an afternoon training session, where I checked the wicket again. It has some grass on top but is bone-dry underneath, the driest I think I've ever seen Lord's. We'll have to work our backsides off again, with bat and ball, to get the result we need. First-innings runs will be absolutely paramount.

The players have been told what the eleven is for tomorrow's match, and I have to sort out the batting order. We'll announce it at the toss, after which we get to meet the Queen, which everyone in the team is very excited about. There's nothing like the Lord's Test match.

Ed Cowan and Mitchell Starc have been replaced by Usman Khawaja and Ryan Harris. Eddie was unlucky to have been brought down by that virus in Nottingham, and the selectors have decided to give Usman a chance. It's been a long road back for him since his last Test match, against New Zealand in Hobart a couple of summers back. He's a good young player who has learnt a lot about his game under Darren Lehmann since moving from New South Wales to Queensland, and I'm really pleased for him.

At the same time, it's hard to see players get dropped. I get on really well with Ed, so I feel for him. But he's a realist and understands he hasn't performed as well as he'd have liked. If I know one thing about him, it's that he'll fight his hardest to get back into the team.

As with Usman, it's also been a hard trek back into the team – in a completely different way – for 'Rhino'.

Ryan played his last Test cricket for us in the West Indies more than a year ago, and I'm sure he would have enhanced his super record at this level if not for the injuries that have brought him down. He wasn't 100 per cent fit for the First Test, which was why he didn't play. Once he'd proved his fitness in the nets, he's our number one Test bowler. His statistics indicate that. He has an unbelievable record. I can't wait to hand him the new ball and see how he goes.

I did my full pre-match press conference, and feel, from my point of view, that I've ruled a line under the Mickey Arthur stuff. That may not satisfy the media, but for me it's over. I can focus on cricket now – which feels like a refuge.

I'm looking forward to contributing a few runs.

Thursday 18 July. London.

It's been yet another cracking day for the cricket fan, though as Australian captain I have mixed feelings. After getting three early wickets I would have liked to be batting by the end of today; but on the other hand, with us losing the toss and Ian Bell making a fine century, it could have been a lot worse.

The warm sunshine had Lord's feeling even more special than usual, if that's possible. This is my Third Test match here, and the more used to it I am, the more

I appreciate the atmosphere, the history, everything about it.

When I took a look at the wicket before the toss, I thought that if there was going to be anything in it, it would be in the first session. It wasn't rock hard under my spikes. Most of the grass had been taken off since earlier in the week, but it was certainly firmer than Trent Bridge, and that hint of moisture had me thinking that if I lost the toss, it wouldn't be the end of the world.

Which I duly did. Watto and I won all four tosses in the Indian Test matches, so I'm probably due for a change in fortune. I called heads again, and lost again. Alastair said he would bat, which I would have done too, but I felt optimistic we could repeat our effort from day one in Nottingham.

An important ritual before the Lord's Test is to meet Her Majesty the Queen. The main thing drilled into the team is how to speak to her. For me, as captain, this meant bowing my head when introduced, and to address her as 'Your Majesty' the first time and 'Ma'am', rhyming with 'Am' not 'Arm', from then onwards. We lined up on the field; the boys found it nerve-racking, but it was great for me to see the excitement on their faces as I introduced them by name and they got a chance to meet her. She was pretty brisk yet gracious, not saying too much. I wasn't too nervous. I was rapt to meet her again. Any opportunity to meet the Queen is one you'll always remember.

THE SECOND TEST MATCH

Then the game got under way, 15 minutes later than usual due to the royal visit.

There was immediately some lateral movement in the air and off the wicket, and Jimmy Pattinson wasn't able to get it in the right areas. In his first two overs, too many balls were hooping away well wide of the off stump, or he'd bowl too close to Cook's body and get turned away to the on side.

During Patto's second over, Hadds turned to me and said, 'What do you reckon about Watto?' Jimmy really wasn't challenging them enough, and one thing about Watto is that he demands the batsmen play. We didn't want both England openers to be leaving so many balls. We also know that Cook doesn't like facing Watto.

So my instructions to him were to attack the stumps and try to get Cook LBW or caught behind, and he delivered the goods second ball, swinging one in late and trapping Cook in front.

The slope at Lord's can play on your mind, both as a batsman and a bowler. You need to take it into consideration, but not get carried away by it. Ryan Harris was bowling from the Pavilion end, which meant the slope was going away from his left to right. That is, it would help the ball going in to the right-handed batsman (and going away from the left-hander); but it also might help him because he has the ability to take the ball away from the batsmen up the hill, which can be the most dangerous ball of all here.

Ryan was simply outstanding. He rifled one through Joe Root that hit the front pad just before hitting his bat. The umpire gave him out, and Root had the decision reviewed, but there was so little in it that the original decision had to stand. As we've seen in the past week, this is a game of millimetres, and the close decisions can go either way.

Rhino is a relentless bowler, and he can be a nightmare for a new batsman because he hardly ever gives them a loose ball to get off the mark. He was right at Kevin Pietersen, who like most of us is an anxious starter, and drew him into a defensive push which Pietersen sort of wanted to play, but sort of wanted to pull away from. He nicked it, and we had just the start we were after.

Jonathan Trott was in good touch again, with some well-timed fours off his pads, and I rotated the bowlers fairly regularly. I wanted to get Patto into the attack, but he still wasn't quite able to apply pressure with a consistent line and length, so I alternated some short spells between him and Watto. We managed to calm Trott down, and he was a bit lucky to survive when he gloved one onto his shoulder and then popped one in the air off the leading edge, the ball falling short of the slips cordon both times.

Lord's has lost the equivalent of ten days worth of rain in the current heatwave, and the pitch is dry, if not quite as dry as Trent Bridge. For us this meant we were in a bit of a race against the sun, to capitalise on our start before the heat sucked the last bit of life out of the strip.

Trott and Bell got through to lunch, but we've noticed that Trott plays his pull shot without a lot of conviction. Mostly he manages to keep it on the ground, but it looks a bit awkward, and if he hit it in the air it wasn't going over the boundary. I placed Usman Khawaja at deep square leg near the Old Father Time weather vane, about ten metres in from the rope. I really don't like having square leg out, but Usman was there to prey on the batsman's mind rather than specifically for a catch, to let Trott know that he'll get short balls and can't rock onto the front foot every ball.

I'm always encouraging our quicks to use their bouncer. Soon enough, Ryan bowled one – and it didn't get up at all! It went wrong. But Trott played that half-hit pull shot and connected too well, placing it where Uzzy only had to run in and take an easy catch. I ran straight to Ryan, and we were laughing at the fact that it didn't go where it was supposed to go but got the wicket anyway.

With England four down for 127, we were back in the game. Our energy in the field was fantastic. The boys were buzzing after the three early wickets, and the feeling was right where I wanted it to be. But throughout the middle session our bowlers lost their control a bit. Their line was on both sides of the wicket, and their length was sometimes too short, sometimes too full. Ashton Agar was struggling with a sore hip flexor after hurting it diving for a ball, and was probably having a first taste of how tough Test cricket can be. We just weren't tightening the screws, and Bell and Bairstow were able to accumulate the runs. Peter Siddle actually bowled Bairstow for 21, but a replay showed that he'd overstepped by a very small margin. Still, there were no excuses, particularly after all the work we'd done on front-foot no-balls and our zero-tolerance policy. Nobody was feeling the pain more than Sidds.

Towards the end of the day, we were getting a bit desperate and seemed to have lost the advantage. But Sidds bowled a fantastic late spell – no fireworks, but drying up the runs with a succession of dot balls. To batsmen who were well set, this was some achievement.

At Lord's more than most grounds, bowlers prefer certain ends. Ryan and Pete were more comfortable bowling from the Pavilion end, so their outswingers were going against the slope. Ryan can move the ball back in off the wicket, so the chance to nip one in down the slope suited him. Peter was swinging the ball consistently away, and if he'd been coming from the Nursery end the Englishmen would have been able to leave pretty much every ball. From the Pavilion end, they felt they had to play because it might come down the slope at them. He got wickets when batsmen were dragged into playing.

THE SECOND TEST MATCH

I think that spell was what set things up for Steve Smith. In the 77th over, I thought I'd give him a couple of overs of leg-spin from the Nursery end before the second new ball fell due. I won't claim any brilliant strategic vision. I just thought he was worth giving a go. The advantage of bowling out of the back of the hand is that bad balls can still get wickets, because of the extra revs on the ball, and they can catch tired batsmen unawares.

Smithy might not have the accuracy and consistency of a front-line leg-spinner, but he's always had the knack of producing a jaffa. His sixth ball was just that – Bell, on 109, pushed forward, and the ball came off the edge to me at first slip. I just held it, actually. It lodged between the heels of my hands. The catch came slow. As slips catches go, it was an easier one, and I might have caught it a bit lazily.

I'd have been ready to take the new ball, but with Smithy on a roll it was worth riding it. The first ball of the 81st over, he bowled what seemed a loopy full toss to Bairstow, who chipped a catch back down the wicket. On the basis of 'when you're on a good thing, stick to it', I kept bowling him, and another two overs later he got a nick from Prior, with Hadds taking a very good catch. We were in it again. Smithy was very bubbly, as usual, and the boys were all stoked for him. It was a great note to finish on, being able to walk off the field with the glow of three late wickets.

So in the end, after all the ups and downs, the day finished about even. I'd love to have batted on that wicket, which is only going to dry out further over the next few days. Tomorrow morning is going to be crucial – knocking over England's last three wickets and building a big first innings of our own. We had Shane Warne come into the dressing room to sit down and help out a few of the boys, and Steve Waugh popped his head in too. The Lord's Test is a bit of a celebrity magnet. We got a visit from the Socceroos' captain, Lucas Neill, and the actor Hugh Jackman – a complete cricket tragic, who absolutely loves the game – also came in and was smiling away with the boys. I like bringing the younger guys in the team into such company. It's good for them to see how these people, who are so successful in all walks of life – Russell Crowe's been visiting the team, for example – just love their cricket so much. I think it reinforces the players' pride in what they do when they hear that these people would give their right arm, basically, to have a Baggy Green. It keeps things in perspective when you're having a bad day (or even a good day) to be reminded how much this position we are in is respected. And also, I guess, on behalf of cricket, I feel proud that it's held in such high esteem outside the cricket community itself.

We had a few laughs, but when anyone asked me about the game, I was saying how good the wicket looks and how much I'm looking forward to batting on it.

THE SECOND TEST MATCH

Friday 19 July. **London.**

If this tour was going to have a Black Friday, today was it. I really don't know what to say. I've had some disappointing moments in cricket, but this time, as captain – and for this to happen at Lord's, of all places – I'm taking it to heart a lot more. I don't remember ever feeling this low after a day's cricket.

I could never have imagined it going this badly after the start we got. First ball of the day, Ryan Harris got one to nip away from Tim Bresnan, and we had a wicket already. Our plan was to cut off the English tail and get in to bat on a wicket that had plenty of runs in it. You can't start any better than a wicket with the first ball.

Rhino soon had Anderson nicking one, and I was stoked to see the big fella with five wickets, his name going up on the Lord's honour board. Not even greats of the game like Shane Warne have achieved that, and Ryan was well aware of what a moment it was. In this team, we celebrate each other's successes, and there could be no more popular recipient of this honour than Ryan Harris. He may be scared of heights, but he fears no batsman.

On the other hand, Patto was again struggling with his line, giving the batsmen width on both sides of the wicket, and I had to take him off. Due to Anderson having come in as night watchman for Stuart Broad yesterday, England ended up with a pretty strong last–

wicket pair, Broad and Swann, both guys who have made centuries in Test cricket. They got away from us a bit, Swann hitting Ryan for three fours in one over, and not even Watto and Sidds could slow them down. I thought they ended up with about 30 runs more than I was hoping for, after a last-wicket stand of 48.

Broad finally nicked Patto to Brad Haddin, and asked for DRS to review it. So we all had to stand there, halfway to the pavilion, to go through the formality, on the off-chance that an official might make a mistake as bad as the one that let Broad off in Nottingham. We hung around for a couple of minutes before the third umpire confirmed he was out. I don't hold it against a player if he doesn't walk, or even if he asks for a review if he genuinely doesn't think he's out.

Watto and Bucky Rogers went out there and made a good start. The atmosphere in the dressing room felt nervous but confident. We knew what a big day in the series it was. Boof was like the Buddha, sitting on the balcony, listening to the television commentary through his earpiece, totally unruffled.

Lord's has been Chris Rogers' home ground in county cricket, so if anyone was used to the slope it was him. Watto, meanwhile, had a couple of big appeals against him in the first two overs. One was for a catch that came off his hip, not his bat, and then Broad appealed for LBW when he hit him clearly outside the line of the off stump. The English spent a long time

THE SECOND TEST MATCH

debating whether to review, which can plant a seed of anxiety in a batsman's head.

But our guys responded well. Watto began patiently, and then took 21 runs off two overs from Anderson and Bresnan, all through the off side. Graeme Swann was off the field, having been hit in the arm, and there was a strong sense that this was our day. Anderson switched to bowling around the wicket to Chris, but drifted onto the pads and was clipped away. Swann came back on just before lunch, but Watto and Chris were into their rhythm now, and it looked like they were going to come into the break together and put us all in high spirits.

In the last over before lunch, Cook switched Bresnan from the Nursery to the Pavilion end. There had not seemed enough time for that over, but Swann had got through his quickly. What a crucial twist it turned out to be. Bresnan bowled three inswingers to Watto, obviously going for the LBW, but he either let them go or laid bat on them. Then, on the fourth ball of the over, Bresnan ducked one in and hit him on the front pad. The umpire gave it out. We've talked a lot about getting our DRS reviews right, but basically there's no other way than trusting the two guys out there, the batsman and the non-striker. Shane thought it was sliding down leg, and he talked to Chris, who said he agreed that it was questionable.

They're both experienced cricketers, Shane and Chris, and I back them if they think it is worth reviewing.

But only part of the ball has to be hitting the stumps to uphold the onfield umpire's decision, and this was what Hawk-Eye said was going to happen – by millimetres, again. It was desperately disappointing.

Still, we had 42 runs on the board, and it was only one wicket. Chris and Usman Khawaja got ready to go out again. Resilience is something we've talked about since India – not letting one or two wickets panic the rest of the batsmen into a collapse. We all know that a big part of mental strength is being able to forget what's gone before, and just treat the present moment for itself.

Unfortunately, Watto's dismissal had a knock-on effect after lunch. Swann was bowling to Chris from the Nursery end, and the ball must have slipped out of his hand. It came out as a high full toss, angled down the leg side, but Chris missed it. The ball hit him in the box, and it didn't look anywhere near out. But such a weird happening must have unhinged everyone a little. Umpire Erasmus gave it out, and Chris and Usman had a chat. We were thinking they had to refer it. But Usman mustn't have got a very clear view of it, as Swann was bowling on a big angle across him from around the wicket, and from Chris' point of view, if he reviewed this and it proved to be out, he would have been party to us losing both of our DRS reviews and we were only two wickets down. So he did the unselfish thing and decided not to review, when the replays showed the ball

THE SECOND TEST MATCH

clearly missing the stumps. All I can put it down to is both the batsmen and the umpire being thrown off-kilter by such a bizarre ball.

Usman soon edged one from Swann straight to slip, where, luckily for us, Jonathan Trott put it down. If we felt that the rub of the green was turning our way, we were soon put back in our place. Phil Hughes went up from number six to four in this match, and I moved from four to five. Two days ago, I sat with Darren Lehmann and discussed the best order for that wicket at Lord's. It's been said that I prefer number five because I have better Test stats there, but the number I bat is irrelevant to me. I've batted number four my whole career at New South Wales and made a few runs. The number has no impact. It is all about what is best for the team in the specific circumstances, and taking into account the wicket itself.

After that discussion, I told Hughesy. Like me, he's not bothered where he bats. At any rate, he flashed at a wide ball from Bresnan, and was given out caught behind. He didn't feel anything, and reviewed it, but the third umpire didn't have enough evidence to overturn the onfield umpire's decision.

Throughout, I waited in the dressing room on the first floor of the pavilion. When the decision was confirmed, I made my way down. It's pretty nerve-racking going out to bat at 3/53 at any time, but at Lord's it's unique, coming down the internal stairs and then walking through all the members in the Long Room. They usually clap and say a few words, not always encouraging, but I was just shutting it all out. I never pay attention to anything as I walk out to bat.

That includes what the fieldsmen were saying. They've said something to me every time I've walked out, but I don't hear it. Usman and I shared a few words of general support, and he faced the next five balls from Swann before taking a single. I had one from Swann, which I defended to the on side. Next over, ultra-keen to rotate the strike, Usman called me through for a very quick single and I was nearly run out when Bairstow's throw hit the stumps. The umpire called for a replay, but I was safely in.

Over the next 10–15 minutes, I felt I was in really good touch. The wicket was allowing the ball to come onto the bat much truer and quicker than at Trent Bridge, and I was middling it well. This was a beautiful batting track, it was a fine, warm day, and it was all laid out for us. We were trying to be positive, but soon, facing Swann, Usman came down the wicket to loft a drive. He got it on the toe of the bat and it flew to mid-off. That meant 4/69, and a bit more pressure.

I was still feeling good, though. Cook brought on Broad to replace Bresnan from the Pavilion end, and he overpitched, allowing me to drive him twice. One straight drive ran into the stumps at the other end, but the other went for four when Bresnan, at mid-off, dived

THE SECOND TEST MATCH

for it too late. Broad stopped the game to make some sort of minute changes to the field. So I backed off and adjusted my gloves, to bring the game back to my timetable.

After the drinks break, Broad went at me with some bouncers, but wasn't very accurate. One went high over my head, and another was a long hop which I was able to punch away through the off side. I was stressing to Smithy that we had to build a partnership and play each ball on its merits.

Sometimes you get yourself out, but with Smithy he got a good ball. Just as he was settling down, he played forward at Swann and it jumped off the track. It hadn't done that at all at Trent Bridge. The ball hit his bat handle and popped to Bell at bat-pad. We were 5/86, and Hadds and I were looking at a rescue job.

I lost a bit of concentration after Smithy got out. England were on top, and I thought I had to drag some momentum back. I told myself to play with good intent and put it back on the bowlers.

Broad was dropping short again, and I pulled one for four. He banged another ball in so short that umpire Dharmasena called it wide for being too high. Then he bowled me a half-volley on my leg stump that I missed. Just a mental error, a lapse of concentration. My game is based around playing straight and I tried to hit it too square and was out LBW. So I was back in the dressing room with the other guys. It was unacceptable after making a good start. In getting out, I'd done everything I'd been telling the boys we had to guard against. I have no excuses. On a wicket like this, when you make a start as I did, you have to cash in. I let a big score go.

By tea, we were seven down. It was a reminder of the middle session at The Oval in 2009: one bad session can lose you a whole match. This was what we've planned against, what we've worked so hard to prevent happening again, and here it is. I wish I had an answer. Believe me, it's not for want of trying.

This time, there was no last-wicket stand to pull us out of the pit we'd dug. We were all out for 128. I gathered the boys together when we went back onto Lord's, and thought about what I might say to show them there was some light at the end of the tunnel. I reminded them that at Cape Town a couple of years back, where a few of us had been involved, South Africa were in a similar position to where we were now, and they'd bowled us out for 47. It's cricket: anything's possible! If we bowl England out cheaply, we're right in this, chasing something like what we so nearly got, on a much harder wicket, in Nottingham. There is a way to win.

The bowlers really went at it positively. Watto had Joe Root edging early, but unfortunately Hadds and I both thought the other guy had it, and neither of us moved. Still, Patto and especially Sidds bowled fantastic spells and brought us back into the game by dismissing Cook, Trott and Pietersen. We've got England's best three batsmen and they're only 30. There is a way to win this – we have to believe.

It's the type of optimism for which Shane Warne was renowned. He could talk everyone around him into believing a win was possible. Tonight, Kyly and I went out to dinner with Shane and his close friends and family. Shane's father Keith was there, and it was a double celebration: Keith's 70th birthday, and Shane being inducted into the ICC Cricket Hall of Fame today. When it happened during a break in play, I made sure the whole team came out onto the balcony to applaud him. It's a special event. Warnie is very modest about his achievements, but I am extremely happy for him. If there's one guy who's earnt the accolade, it's him. I know inside he was proud.

Now that I've sat down to think about today, though, it's hit me again how horrible our batting was. Horrendous, on a good wicket. If we're not careful, it will cost us this Test match and a lot more. Some of our top six got starts but didn't go on, and we're nowhere near consistent enough to beat good teams when we play like this. Put simply, the batting group has let the team down. The bowlers are fighting, but no bowlers are good enough to keep knocking teams over for a hundred, which is what we're effectively asking them to do, particularly if they've only got 50 overs of wet between innings.

It's unacceptable.

Saturday 20 July. London.

Another bad day, really, even though there were no disasters. We've been left in a terrible predicament by the way we batted yesterday.

England patiently manoeuvred themselves into position. I gathered the boys together again and tried to keep their optimism up. If we took seven wickets in the first session, we would be chasing around 350 to win, with plenty of time. That was the way forward.

But Joe Root and Tim Bresnan played well, and we couldn't find a chink in their armour. The missed chance yesterday when Root was on 8 has turned out to be really costly. He's 178 not out now.

There's not a lot to say about today's play. It was much cooler, and I was in my sweater all day. The wicket's still very good. The hardest thing for the bowlers was that they know our success is based on building pressure through maiden overs, but they were also fighting impatience – the need to get England out quickly to have a chance of winning. Every run was crucial. So finding that balance between attack and containment was difficult.

There was a bit of swing for the bowlers, and after we got Bresnan, we hoped to spark a collapse, but Ian Bell had a bit of luck. He chipped Ryan Harris somehow just over short mid-wicket, but short of mid-on. You couldn't do that if you tried. My hands were on my head and I was gasping in frustration.

THE SECOND TEST MATCH

Straight after, Bell edged Harris for a regulation catch to Steve Smith at gully. Because it was caught low to the ground, though, it went up to the third umpire. The officials are not meant to be swayed by this kind of thing, but I felt we might have influenced events by not celebrating more exuberantly. We were all a bit uncertain at first. Ryan didn't jump up and down, and Steve said he thought he'd caught it, but wasn't throwing the ball up and carrying on. I walked over to Steve and said, 'Did you catch it?'

He thought he had and I thought he'd caught it too.

When we looked at the replay, it was pretty straightforward: he'd got his fingers under the ball. It was another blow when Tony Hill, the third umpire, said he could not give it out because he thought he had seen some contact between the ball and the ground.

England continued to bat all day. I gave Root a good clap when he reached his 150, as he'd played very well, but the game was drifting. To be honest, I was very surprised that they didn't declare before stumps, giving themselves about six overs to go at us with the new ball and try to take a wicket when we were tired and dulled from a day in the field. They just seemed to want us to keep on bowling.

My priority, in the last hour, was to preserve our pacemen. They were stuffed. I didn't have any choice. With three Test matches to play, my priority is not destroying our bowlers. So I didn't take the new ball, instead giving Ashton Agar and Steve Smith a long spell together. The game sort of coasted towards the end of the day, without much action.

Now that I'm sitting in my room, I don't even know how many runs England are in front. That says something about the bad position we're in. But you never know. If we bat for two days, we'll win the Test match. It's one tough ask, but what I do know is that as a batting unit we're well and truly due, me especially. Let's hope that a few of us put our hands up.

Sunday 21 July. **London.**

This afternoon, once the match was finished, I was interviewed on the ground at Lord's for television. Thousands of people were still in the stands. I said I believed we could still win the series from 0–2 down. People laughed.

I can see where they're coming from, but we have the talent to do it. England are a good side, but the scoreline is not a fair reflection of the difference between the teams. Once we beat them, we'll believe we can win the series – I strongly believe that when we get to that point we'll be hard to stop. Having fallen just short at Trent Bridge is looking more and more costly. It was only 15 runs, but in confidence it would have been worth a great deal more.

THE SECOND TEST MATCH

Every loss is tough, whether it's a near-miss at Trent Bridge or a sound thrashing here. I take it more personally as captain, and it hurts me to see these guys I care so much about feeling so miserable, but I have to say I've *hated* losing whenever it's happened to me as an Australian Test player, captain or not. Hated it.

When we arrived at Lord's today, we came with an open mind. The confidence was there. Having seen England score plenty of runs, we knew that if we batted long enough we would get enough. It was going to be hard with the footmarks and the ball spinning, but we thought if we fought our way through the tough spells, we had the skill to win this, despite what history might say.

We removed Bairstow and Root pretty quickly, and Cook declared after only about half an hour's play. Such an early declaration confirmed my surprise over why he hadn't left time to have a crack at us yesterday afternoon.

It was cool and cloudy when Watto and Bucky started out. Again, they looked perfectly comfortable against the new ball. There was swing for Broad and Anderson, but nothing our openers couldn't handle.

Then Watto was out LBW – another close one, but out. Swann was brought on soon after, from the Nursery end. He had some craggy footmarks to bowl into, as the pitch was harder than Nottingham and all the pacemen from both sides are right-armers, so there were deep craters outside the left-handed batsmen's off stump. Bowling from that end, he would be turning the ball away from the slope, but running it downhill when he bowled his top-spinner.

He deceived Chris with a beautiful piece of bowling – the big turner that flew sideways out towards slip, and a couple of balls later the arm ball that missed the footmarks, skidded down the slope and glanced Chris' off stump. You have to credit the bowler for something like that. Swann had got Chris with one of the worst balls ever in the first innings, but he'd balanced that out with a fine piece of bowling now.

Hughesy joined Usman, but not for long. I saw Swann's LBW appeal against Phillip and the umpire gave him out. I put my helmet on, put my gloves on, and picked up my bat. The replay came on, and the other guys in the changing room told me it was out. I was on my way, down through the Long Room again. On the fourth day, a reciprocity arrangement means that Sydney Cricket Ground members are in the pavilion at Lord's. The support we've had from Australians and English people has been outstanding. I'm amazed at how many English supporters want us to beat England! It's nice to hear when you're on the other side of the world.

I went out in a sleeveless vest against the cooler weather, and set myself to play positively. I've always used my feet to the spinners, and it's brought me success, so I saw no reason to change against Swann. With Mitchell Starc not having played, there were no footmarks outside my off stump. On the seventh ball I faced, I went down

THE SECOND TEST MATCH

the track and Swann's delivery went dead straight. I played inside the line and got a nick. That nick saved me. The ball deviated a little and hit Matt Prior's knee, bouncing clear before he could catch or stump me. Some luck going my way – I *had* to make the most of it.

Soon I felt that my footwork was upsetting Swann's length. He bowled me a full toss, which I hit through cover down the hill for four. I got some runs off Bresnan, who was tight but not threatening, and asked for some new gloves. My hands really sweat up when I'm nervous.

Uzzy and I got us through to lunch. James Anderson chose to walk beside me as I went towards the pavilion, murmuring pleasantries – 'Good luck', and all that (and pigs might fly). After lunch, Broad was brought on from the Pavilion end to bowl some short ones, but Uzzy forced him through the on side a couple of times and I got some runs too. On the dying wicket, bouncers might not have seemed a smart plan of attack, but all opposition teams now try it on me, and Broad seems to be the chosen guy here.

In Swann's next over, Usman called for a single and I ran through. When I looked around, Swann was writhing on the ground and Usman was apologising. I didn't see it, but Usman had got him – accidentally – with a solid bump. Graeme might have been affected, because for the next little while Usman and I both got a fair few runs off him. It was a good battle, especially when he forced me back, but I was determined not to let him dictate, so I got down the wicket and hit him over mid-on for a four on the first bounce. He put a deep mid-on in place two-thirds of the way back to the boundary, which was a win for me, as I could then knock the ball down there along the ground for easy singles.

From the Pavilion end, meanwhile, Broad was bowling to a fairly predictable short-pitched strategy. What wasn't predictable was how the ball bounced. Lord's was definitely quicker than Trent Bridge, but as we saw on the first day when Ryan Harris' bouncer to Trott didn't get up, it was hard to judge how high the bounce was. I didn't feel comfortable ducking, in case the ball didn't get up. So with one of Broad's bouncers, I just stood there and it caught me hard on the upper left arm. Another, I went back to defend and it shot through and got me in the ribs, just below my heart. And then, when I stood to block the next ball, it leapt up and caught me on the helmet, flush on the Australian badge.

Another got me on the left hip and Broad appealed, but he was also wasting a lot of bouncers down the leg side, and when he tried to pitch it up, he wasn't executing very well. We could see he was feeling the tension: when Usman pulled his slower bouncer for four, Broad gave Trott at square leg an absolute gobful.

The thing was, we were surviving, and putting some runs on the board. Anderson came on to replace Broad from the Pavilion end, and I felt more comfortable against him than at Trent Bridge. He was covering the ball with his left hand, his usual practice when he's bowling reverse swing, but it wasn't doing as much as it had in Nottingham. I ran one off the face of the bat to third man for four, got on my toes for a cut through cover point, and generally defended him pretty well.

Usman was getting a lot of the strike to Swann, but he was batting really well now, getting away the odd boundary. We got the score up into the 100s, then the 110s – not that the score was paramount, but it eased the pressure to be putting on runs while also defending staunchly.

After drinks, Swann switched to bowl around the wicket to me, hoping to get something going out of the footmarks. But he was bowling enough loose ones for me to either get a single away or hit a four, mainly by getting down the wicket and driving through cover. Usman, at the other end, hauled Swann away to deep mid-wicket for three, and then clipped Anderson neatly away for four.

In the 44th over, when the score was 3/119, Cook brought on Joe Root with his off-spinners. It's something I've often done when a bloke has made a big score with the bat: he feels he can do no wrong, and can jag a wicket with the ball. Uzzy dealt with him okay, though, except for one where they appealed for a catch at slip – another delivery that exploded out of the footmarks at a radical angle without the bat having hit it.

After we'd seen off Anderson, Bresnan was brought back again. He bowled two ordinary balls wide of my off stump that I threw my hands at in a slightly uncontrolled way. One went over slips, and I was eyeing the gap behind point when I inside-edged the next and nearly chopped it onto my stumps. Concentrate!

Root, like Swann, was coming around the wicket to me. Cook put himself at leg slip, and it was fairly obvious that they would try to aim at or outside my leg stump. I knew that was how they wanted to get me out. Root had put his first ball to me in that spot, and I went back and turned it around the corner for a single. When he tossed it up there again, I should have played back, not forward, but in a lazy moment, I selected the wrong shot and glanced it off the front foot – straight to Cook.

I bowed over my bat, disappointed beyond belief. We'd fought so hard, and here it was me letting the side down. Again.

Usman was out in Root's next over. You hate it when a part-timer takes wickets, because it gives the fielding side a lift and a laugh and it shows that you haven't placed a high enough price on your wicket. I wouldn't say that about Usman, who batted tremendously well, but I will about myself. Just lazy.

The lower order, as usual, put up some resistance. Smith and Agar were out to what looked like speculative decisions from the third umpire, but it's a cop-out to blame the DRS and I won't do it. We weren't lucky, but we weren't good enough to make our own luck. At the end of the day, Jimmy Pattinson and Ryan Harris stuck

THE SECOND TEST MATCH

around to make the English come back tomorrow, but the play was extended and a couple of balls before the end, Jimmy was last man out.

It's hard to swallow back your disappointment at these moments, but as captain I have to press on. Matt Cenin, our media liaison, took me to the Nursery end to have a press conference, which I can't possibly enjoy after a loss.

As captain, though, I'm the team's public face, and our creed of keeping the highest standards applies to media duties as much as everything else. I was asked some interesting questions, as usual, some about the quality of our batting. I said: 'You learn defence at the age of ten. Some of the best innings I've seen are Test centuries off 350 balls. I don't want people to not back their natural instincts, but when you're playing good opposition there will be tough times. You need your defence to get through that.' That's no different from what we've been telling the boys. It's just a matter of putting it into action consistently. There's a lot of talk about how Twenty20 cricket is affecting batsmen's technique and concentration, but I don't think that applies to any Australian Test cricketers. That said, there's no dodging the main issue, which is that we batsmen must hold ourselves accountable for what's happened. 'We're letting our bowlers down by not putting enough runs on the board,' I said.

As usual, I was asked how much it hurt to lose. I don't really know what to say. You can't put it into words. You try to think of another way of saying essentially the same thing. I said, 'It hurt me just as much when I was a player, not captain. You play to win. I was lucky to start my career in a great Australian team, and winning was a habit that I became accustomed to. I don't want that to change.'

I was told that the last Australian captain to lose six straight Test matches was Kim Hughes, who resigned in tears in 1984. The questioner, John Townsend from *The West Australian*, said, 'I presume that's not going to happen.' I cut in with a throwaway line – 'Presume nothing!' – which gave everybody a lighter moment, and sure, who knows what the future holds? But I'd never known of that stat, and I'm certainly not about to quit as captain.

I understand that as captain I'm accountable for the team's results. So if we continue to play the way we're playing, and if there's somebody better to captain Australia, replacing me is a decision for Cricket Australia to make. I'm not thinking about that, though. I'm thinking about how to make more runs and help the team win. Every day I'm thinking about how I can score more runs. If I'm dropped as captain or a player, I'll deal with that at the time, but I'm trying not to think about it.

Monday 22 July. **London. Afternoon.**

Today, what was meant to be the fifth day of the Lord's Test match, was a day off. For me right now, a 'day off'

THE SECOND TEST MATCH

means a day of treatment. I started with a session on the MedX machine and some physio work from Alex, and later a massage from Grant Baldwin. Grant, by the way, won Boof's pink jacket for the 'one-percenters' at Lord's, while Rhino Harris wore the cream blazer for man of the match. My back's a bit stiff and sore. It felt really stiff yesterday before we went back out into the field, and after batting it was still sore. It's not only my back, either. I've spent much of the day lying on my bed with three icepacks on my body: on my ribs, my left shoulder and on my left hip.

I've found it hard to switch my mind off. I had a drink with some mates last night, and it was good to be brought out of myself and have a laugh, but when I'm on my own or in treatment, it's hard to escape the harsh truth. Losing six Tests is obviously a record I don't want to be part of. I'll be doing everything in my power to make sure it's not seven in a row.

Any time you lose it hurts. The way we play, we'll win games and lose games. The hardest thing to accept is how often we're not winning. For myself, my prime responsibility to the team is scoring runs. I want to go to Hove to play our three-day match against Sussex this week. I need more time in the middle, and want to score some runs to take confidence to Old Trafford. I'm accountable for my poor shot selection in both innings here at Lord's. This team expects me to convert starts into a good score. I do believe we're good enough to win this series. I want to give the team confidence and score a lot more runs than I have so far.

When I get low like this, it helps to talk to Kyly and my family. Dad's over his knee replacement, and is back home on the couch watching plenty of Test cricket. He doesn't miss a ball, and is sending me messages every day. All my close family know how much I hate not performing as well as I want, so they're offering every encouragement. It does help.

Monday 22 July. **London. Night.**

We've just come back from team drinks and dinner, where the wives and partners were welcome, and it was good to see everyone in good spirits. But I also just got the news that James Pattinson has a stress fracture in his back and has been pulled out of the series. We're hoping that he can be rested and managed so that he's ready for the Australian summer.

Jimmy will be around the group through Sussex and Old Trafford, and then he'll fly home out of Manchester. I really feel for him. Things haven't gone to plan for him, with some good spells alternating with frustrating ones. Most of all, as part of the batting group, I feel responsible for a situation where he's had to bowl every day of the series. We just haven't batted long enough to give him and the other seamers a rest. I'm just gutted for him.

THE SECOND TEST MATCH

Tuesday 23 July. **Brighton.**

We've driven down to Brighton, to stay at the beachfront Hilton Brighton Metropole Hotel – a nice change of scenery, and refreshing for all us Aussies who like the coast. We're lighter in number than usual, as four of the support staff – plus Chris Rogers, Ryan Harris, Shane Watson and Peter Siddle – have stayed in London. Darren allowed them to stay and freshen up and do some training there. Some of them will head to Sussex to join us in the next couple of days, while others will go straight to Manchester and meet us there.

I'm struggling with pain of more than one kind. For six or seven days now, I've had a persistent pain in my left hip. This morning before getting on the bus, I had a cortisone injection in my hip joint. It had better improve. At the moment, I can't feel my left quad, so it's awkward walking around. I've also still got some back soreness from the Lord's Test match. Being hunched over at slip for long periods has stirred it up. In the next few days, I have to allow my body to recover so I can get back on the park for the Third Test.

The frustration – with everything – is growing. I don't mind my body being sore after scoring hundreds. Right now, I've got the soreness but not the results.

I keep trying to remind myself that as a leader I have to look beyond the here and now, the waves smashing into us every day. My eyes also have to be focused on the horizon. Rather than getting dragged down by the frustration I'm feeling with this pain on this day, I have to set my mind upon this whole series and getting back into it – and on the future too: to our objective, as a squad, of becoming as good as we can be and regaining our status as number one in the world.

That's what I'm using to take my mind off the present buffeting.

It's easier said than done.

Second Test
18 July 2013. Lord's, London.

England (first innings)

Batting		R	B	4	6	SR
AN Cook	lbw: Watson	12	14	2	0	85.71
JE Root	lbw: Harris	6	14	1	0	42.86
IJL Trott	c: Khawaja b: Harris	58	87	11	0	66.67
KP Pietersen	c: Haddin b: Harris	2	4	0	0	50.00
IR Bell	c: Clarke b: Smith	109	211	16	0	51.66
JM Bairstow	c&b: Smith	67	146	7	0	45.89
MJ Prior	c: Haddin b: Smith	6	18	1	0	33.33
TT Bresnan	c: Haddin b: Harris	7	29	1	0	24.14
JM Anderson	c: Haddin b: Harris	12	29	2	0	41.38
SCJ Broad	c: Haddin b: Pattinson	33	29	5	1	113.79
GP Swann	not out	28	26	5	0	107.69
	Extras (11lb, 4w, 6nb, 0b)	21				
	Total 10 Wkts, 100.1 Overs	361			3.60 Runs/Over	

Bowling	O	M	R	W	Econ	SR	Extras
JL Pattinson	20.1	3	95	1	4.71	121.0	(4w, 3nb)
RJ Harris	26.0	6	72	5	2.77	31.2	
SR Watson	13.0	4	45	1	3.46	78.0	
PM Siddle	22.0	6	76	0	3.45		(1nb)
AC Agar	13.0	2	44	0	3.38		(2nb)
SPD Smith	6.0	1	18	3	3.00	12.0	

Australia (first innings)

Batting		R	B	4	6	SR
SR Watson	lbw: Bresnan	30	42	6	0	71.43
CJL Rogers	lbw: Swann	15	45	0	0	33.33
UT Khawaja	c: Pietersen b: Swann	14	35	1	0	40.00
PJ Hughes	c: Prior b: Bresnan	1	8	0	0	12.50
MJ Clarke	lbw: Broad	28	41	4	0	68.29
SPD Smith	c: Bell b: Swann	2	14	0	0	14.29
BJ Haddin	c: Trott b: Swann	7	42	1	0	16.67
AC Agar	run out (Prior)	2	21	0	0	9.52
PM Siddle	c: Swann b: Anderson	2	24	0	0	8.33
JL Pattinson	not out	10	24	1	0	41.67
RJ Harris	c: Pietersen b: Swann	10	25	1	0	40.00
	Extras (1lb, 2w, 0nb, 4b)	7				
	Total 10 Wkts, 53.3 Overs	128			2.39 Runs/Over	

Bowling	O	M	R	W	Econ	SR	Extras
JM Anderson	14.0	8	25	1	1.79	84.0	(1w)
SCJ Broad	11.0	3	26	1	2.36	66.0	(1w)
TT Bresnan	7.0	1	28	2	4.00	21.0	
GP Swann	21.3	5	44	5	2.05	25.8	

England (second innings)

Batting		R	B	4	6	SR
AN Cook	b: Siddle	8	28	0	0	28.57
JE Root	c: Smith b: Harris	180	338	18	2	53.25
IJL Trott	b: Siddle	0	6	0	0	0.00
KP Pietersen	c: Rogers b: Siddle	5	11	1	0	45.45
TT Bresnan	c: Rogers b: Pattinson	38	137	4	0	27.74
IR Bell	c: Rogers b: Smith	74	103	11	0	71.84
JM Bairstow	c: Haddin b: Harris	20	54	2	1	37.04
MJ Prior	not out	1	8	0	0	12.50
SCJ Broad						
GP Swann						
JM Anderson						
	Extras (8lb, 0w, 0nb, 15b)	23				
	Total 7 Wkts, 114.1 Overs	349		3.06 Runs/Over		

Bowling	O	M	R	W	Econ	SR	Extras
RJ Harris	18.1	4	31	2	1.71	54.5	
SR Watson	12.0	5	25	0	2.08		
PM Siddle	21.0	6	65	3	3.10	42.0	
JL Pattinson	20.0	8	42	1	2.10	120.0	
SPD Smith	14.0	0	65	1	4.64	84.0	
AC Agar	29.0	5	98	0	3.38		

Australia (second innings)

Batting		R	B	4	6	SR
SR Watson	lbw: Anderson	20	23	3	0	86.96
CJL Rogers	b: Swann	6	29	0	0	20.69
UT Khawaja	c: Anderson b: Root	54	133	7	0	40.60
PJ Hughes	lbw: Swann	1	21	0	0	4.76
MJ Clarke	c: Cook b: Root	51	85	7	0	60.00
SPD Smith	c: Prior b: Bresnan	1	14	0	0	7.14
BJ Haddin	lbw: Swann	7	32	0	0	21.88
AC Agar	c: Prior b: Bresnan	16	13	4	0	123.08
PM Siddle	b: Anderson	18	62	1	0	29.03
JL Pattinson	lbw: Swann	35	91	3	0	38.46
RJ Harris	not out	16	40	1	0	40.00
	Extras (5lb, 1w, 0nb, 4b)	10				
	Total 10 Wkts, 90.3 Overs	235		2.60 Runs/Over		

Bowling	O	M	R	W	Econ	SR	Extras
JM Anderson	18.0	2	55	2	3.06	54.0	
SCJ Broad	21.0	4	54	0	2.57		
GP Swann	30.3	5	78	4	2.56	45.8	
TT Bresnan	14.0	8	30	2	2.14	42.0	(1w)
JE Root	7.0	3	9	2	1.29	21.0	

6

THE THIRD TEST MATCH

Wednesday 24 July. Brighton.

I'm not going to play in the game against Sussex, which starts the day after tomorrow. My back is still sore, and a couple of sessions on the MedX machine didn't leave me pain-free. That machine is fast turning into my best mate, but there's only so much it can do. I just need rest.

The hip is a strange one. I don't know how it happened, but it's been with me since the beginning of the tour, and about six days ago it became quite painful. The cortisone helped settle it down. But it's hard not to conclude that the pains in the hip and back, all around that pelvic area, are related.

Instead of training, I went to the Hove ground with the team and talked to the batsmen individually. Our focus is on how to face Graeme Swann and possibly Monty Panesar at Old Trafford, where traditionally the ball spins more. Going by what we've seen already in the series, we can expect a dry pitch prepared to help them. At the nets I spoke with each of the batsmen, and I had a further chat with Phil Hughes back at our hotel on the Brighton seafront.

The essence of it was, everyone's different, but you have to have your own plan and back it 100 per cent, rain, hail or shine. Work on it at the nets and in your free time. Then, use the county games to work on it further. My plan is firstly to use my feet, but not everyone bats like that, and the last thing we want is for guys to go outside their natural style. Some guys like to go back more; others play straight rather than sweep, and others use the sweep shot. Darren is a great sounding board, having been such a terrific improviser against spin bowling. But even though he used different tactics at different times, he too followed his own plan on any given day.

Darren wanted me to stay in London and freshen up with Chris, Shane, Ryan and Peter, but I wanted to come here to recover, talk to the boys, and get back to batting again. Initially, I wanted to have some time in the middle, but a day or so ago we understood that wasn't going to happen here.

THE THIRD TEST MATCH

That said, I'm really enjoying my temporary 'batting coaching' role. It's a nice change to be around the group without the personal pressure of preparing for a match.

Tonight we've had another trivia quiz, and the Clarke group didn't cover itself in glory. Peter Brukner devised a test on 'The Year 2012'. As this is the part of the tour when the wives and partners are travelling with us, they were invited to have their own tables. A table headed by Brad Haddin and Steve Smith won the contest. My group included Matthew Wade, Phillip Hughes, Jackson Bird, and Matt Cenin. And we finished last.

Well, 2012 was a long time ago, when you have a hard time remembering what happened in the last 24 hours!

Thursday 25 July. Brighton.

Today, our last day before the Sussex game, was an optional training day. I wasn't able to train but went anyway, to assist the left-handed batsmen again with their planning on how to face England's spinners.

Some of the boys have been stirring Boof about his reputation as a player of spin. It's just been the usual light-hearted cheekiness, but I guess a lot of the team are too young to have seen him play at his peak, so they have to take it on trust! Anyway, he decided to set the record straight by going into the nets and having a bat.

He might not be in prime physical shape at the age of 43, but he proved one thing, which is that he could walk out and bat for us next week in the Test match.

The boys unpacked their gear at the ground, and there's a lot of excitement in the group. Ashton Turner, a teenage off-spinner and right-handed batsman from Western Australia, will make his first-class debut. Ed Cowan is delighted to be captain, in the absence of myself and Brad Haddin. My job, meanwhile, is to run out some Gatorades and give the batsmen gloves when they need them. Of course I came down here intending to play, but I'm actually looking forward to not having nerves in my system.

After training, I went to the barber's for a haircut. Back at the hotel, we were given a message that we could not leave our rooms or go into the corridors at all, as somebody on our floor had passed away. Our security guard told me it was a 60-year-old man who'd had a heart attack in the bath. It's extremely sad for his family, and when these things happen, it's a reminder that what we're doing, while of the utmost importance to all of us and those who follow cricket, is only a game.

Friday 26 July. **Brighton.**

One thing we have done well on this tour has been to make the most of our county games. On a good wicket at

THE THIRD TEST MATCH

Hove, the boys went about their work very professionally after Ed Cowan won the toss and decided to bat.

Ed and Hughesy made a great start, putting on 150 in a little more than two hours, but yet again neither could go on to make a hundred. We've talked so much about going on and making big scores, there's not much more we can say. Both Ed and Phil had that bittersweet feeling of making good half-centuries, but not the three-figure scores they were after.

The other two Test batsmen had pretty good days. Usman Khawaja batted number three, looked good and made 40, until he nicked one off Monty Panesar. Steve Smith was scratchy at the start, but I was very happy with the way he got through that, and he's there at the end of play on 98 not out. I'm sure he'll be taking a lot of confidence from that to the next Test match, particularly the way he played spin.

Of the others who had a bat, James Faulkner made a very good 48 before getting out to an uncharacteristic shot, losing concentration and slog-sweeping in the second-last over of the day, and poor Matthew Wade made a duck. I really feel for Wadey. As much as you love being part of an Ashes tour, you really want to play. He finally got his chance today, but unfortunately he cut one off Panesar straight to backward point. Poor bugger.

Meanwhile, I ran Gatorades and Hydrolytes for the boys and sat on the balcony and talked cricket. The boys took the mickey out of me being twelfth man, and enjoyed ordering me about, but I have to say I really enjoyed my downtime.

Saturday 27 July. Brighton

Right now I'm sitting in the hotel watching the rain fall over the beach and the sea. Surprisingly, it's quite a nice sight. You wouldn't normally think this in England, but I haven't seen rain for a while, and it's pleasantly relaxing.

The boys managed to fit in about 65 overs of play before the rain finally shut it down.

Feeling good when I woke up, I went to Hove early and got some batting in the nets and slips catching. It was all fine, which is an enormous relief. I was prepared to settle back into my twelfth man duties when I found that I'd been sacked, or something like it. Had I mixed the drinks the wrong way? Gone out with the wrong gloves? No – Boof just thought it was a good idea to send me away from cricket for a couple of hours. He's the boss, so who am I to argue? So Kyly and I went to the movies and saw Hugh Jackman's new film, *The Wolverine*. It was good to get my head out of cricket, but as soon as we came out, I found it too difficult to be away from the boys, so I went back to the ground to watch for a couple of hours.

Steve Smith had made his hundred this morning, and Ed Cowan declared. We have Sussex five down at stumps. From what I saw and heard, Jackson Bird was the pick of the bowlers. Mitchell Starc bowled a good first spell, while the spinners and James Faulkner came back well after being hit around a bit early. England had brought James Taylor from Nottinghamshire into the Sussex team to do a Test trial, in case Kevin Pietersen's calf injury keeps him out of the Old Trafford match. Taylor made an unbeaten 60-odd, but we dropped three or four catches and bowled some front-foot no-balls – so, after the rain came down, our debrief was all about letting out some frustration over those basic errors.

Still, the boys are pretty upbeat and are looking forward to some sunshine and batting time tomorrow.

Sunday 28 July. Brighton to Manchester.

I've just arrived at our hotel in Manchester, having driven up with Brad Haddin and Kyly. I must have done something really bad as twelfth man, because this morning Boof found another reason to get me away from doing that job. He figured that some of us who are not playing in the Sussex match could come up early so we can have an extra day of training tomorrow, when the rest of the team are travelling. Ryan Harris also drove up here with his wife.

We got to watch the first half of the day's play. Sussex batted on for another 35 overs, allowing Taylor to make his hundred, and then we had 44 overs. Ed Cowan made another good score, and Wadey had some time in the middle with the bat, so I'm pleased for both of them. All in all, the game was a good hit-out for both batsmen and bowlers, and the players who have rested will have made the most of that.

The streets of Manchester are wet, which is making me feel hopeful about the wicket at Old Trafford. We've had so many dry ones, so with a lot of rain in the last few days and more forecast, we're hoping to see something resembling a 'traditional English wicket' – if such a thing still exists!

Monday 29 July. Manchester.

It kept raining today, so the five of us who were here had a pretty easy day with some work in the indoor nets at Old Trafford. I did what I'll usually do in these conditions, which is to work on technical stuff with my batting, getting my shape and balance right while facing throwdowns and the bowling machine. By the end of the session, I felt I was going much better than at the start.

After lunch, the rest of the squad arrived after a six-and-a-half-hour bus ride from Brighton. It only took us five hours yesterday, so I can see why they were looking so jaded. Apparently they had terrible traffic to cope with. After they arrived, we all did rehab and recovery, and everyone seemed pretty keen to get an early night.

I'm hoping the sun will come out tomorrow; I'm very eager to see some signs of life in this Old Trafford wicket.

Tuesday July 30. **Manchester.**

The sun came out, thank God, and we had a really good training session. I was happy to see the boys' spirits up again after their draining day on the motorway in the bus yesterday. The batsmen had good sessions on the practice nets, and our slips-catching group had a workout. The bowlers got to use some brand-new balls on the pacy, bouncy practice decks, which everyone enjoyed, but once I saw the centre wicket, I knew it would bear no resemblance to what we're practising on.

Even with all the rain, the wicket is super-dry. It has a little bit of light-brown grass on top, which – how can I say? – looks as if it's been burnt. There is grass, but when you rub the blades between your fingers it's very crispy and powdery. It'll be mown again tomorrow. There are already bare patches, and the rest of the pitch is covered in this strange-looking dead grass.

So, as with the first two Test matches, the best time to bat will be against the new ball and early in the match. I'd say this wicket is the driest of the lot, and with Old Trafford's reputation for taking spin, I'll be very surprised if England don't play two spinners. We'll see how our selectors feel. I don't know yet if Rod and

Darren are leaning towards one or two spinners. But all of our bowlers, apart from Patto of course, are in contention.

After practice, Hadds and I went to do an appearance for Asics, one of Cricket Australia's official sponsors and one of my personal sponsors. They're a good bunch of people and an easy company to deal with, so even though we were required for four hours to do a photo shoot and some media interviews, the afternoon passed enjoyably. Then, for me, it was back to the hotel for room service with Kyly and an early night. It's time to draw myself in and start my last period of preparation for this Test match. We have to win it to keep our chances alive of getting the urn back. That's obvious. What I'm wanting to see is a big improvement on our performance, particularly with the bat in the first innings.

Wednesday 31 July. **Manchester.**

More rain has come in today, though the forecasts are for decent weather during the Test match. We tried to get as much normal training in as possible at the nets, but were soon chased off by showers.

I've thought a lot about how Swann and Root bowled to me at Lord's, and with another spinning wicket on the cards I expect them to come around the

THE THIRD TEST MATCH

wicket again, using the rough, and placing a leg slip. Today I had Nathan Lyon bowling around the wicket on a leg-stump line, and worked on a different plan. The key, I think, is to stay back as much as possible and not force the issue: just wait on the shorter one and tuck it away. One of the things I love about this game is the constant challenges it throws up, even when you're in your 95th Test match.

Shane Warne joined the group at training, and I discussed my plans with him. He is so brilliant on the psychological side of spin bowling, providing great insights into the cut-and-thrust between batsman and bowler in the space between the ears. He's talked to Nathan and Ashton Agar about attitude and how to exude confidence towards the batsman. Nathan is a naturally shy individual and it's been great for him to hear Shane's advice on how to overcome that.

Tonight, Kyly and I went for a quick dinner with Shane, talking about the game and the series so far. I was asking him for anything he's seen in the two matches that can give us an edge. He's a great friend and I value his opinions. Most of all, what he gives me is an injection of self-belief. When I worry about my game, Warnie is saying, 'No, mate, you're creaming them, you'll make a hundred for sure.' When it comes from a player and watcher of his quality and experience, I believe him. I don't think I've ever come out of a conversation with Warnie where I don't have a smile on my face and am walking a bit taller, ready to face whatever or whoever. He's a fantastic mentor and motivator. I wish I could carry that confidence with me every day of my life.

The selectors have made three changes, bringing in David Warner, Nathan Lyon and Mitchell Starc for Phillip Hughes, Ashton Agar and James Pattinson. Hughesy is unlucky, but Davey scored by all accounts a very good 193 against South Africa A and he's a confidence player, so there's a possibility that he can really take hold of the game when the bowlers are tired. Nathan has continued to work hard on his bowling while out of the Test team, and I think that with the tuition Shane Warne has been giving him, he's going to be a new bowler. Starcy won the third seamer's position ahead of Jackson Bird because we think he can bowl that wicket-taking ball at the start of the innings, and exploit the reverse swing when the shine comes off. His footmarks might also gouge up the turf outside the right-handers' off stump, providing an opportunity for Nathan.

Off to bed now, and hoping for some sunshine tomorrow.

Thursday 1 August. **Manchester.**

Well, that's better! It's too early to say whether today is a turning point in the series. I'm still keeping an eye on the horizon, and the way I think of it is, we're wanting

THE THIRD TEST MATCH

to improve our performance as a batting group and today was a step in that direction.

The players in the team who knew cricket administrator Graham Dixon wore black armbands for him. Graham passed away this week. He was a very popular chief executive of Queensland Cricket, and we feel it's important to recognise and respect people like Graham who have contributed so much to our game.

For me it was a satisfying day, first of all because I won the toss. Losing the toss at Trent Bridge and Lord's hasn't been critical, I didn't think – there were enough in the conditions in both matches to make batting first difficult. We proved that by dismissing England relatively cheaply both times. But here, it was a big toss to win. The pitch is very flat, and it looks like the type of game where runs will be easier to make in the first innings.

'Easier' never means 'easy' in Test cricket, though. Chris Rogers and Shane Watson got us off to a very pleasing start, as they have done throughout the series. Shane has been working on a few elements of his technique, and he wasn't as aggressive as usual. Chris was the one who took the lead, driving beautifully through the off side. He dominated the partnership before Watto was out nicking Bresnan to slip.

Then we had another DRS drama. Uzzy Khawaja had only just started, when he played and missed at a Swann ball turning away from him. The English appealed, and Tony Hill gave him out, but Usman asked for a review.

I was getting myself ready to go out and bat, but it was pretty clear from the replays that he hadn't hit it. The job of the third umpire in this situation is to uphold the onfield umpire's decision unless there is clear evidence to overturn it. The replay showed daylight between the bat and the ball, Hot Spot showed no mark on Usman's edge, and the sound that had prompted the appeal was caused by Usman's bat brushing his own leg. So I was extremely frustrated when Kumar Dharmasena gave him out. It came at a bad time for us, just before lunch, and was particularly hard for Usman, a young batsman who had a chance to place his stamp on the game. And it left us down to our last unsuccessful DRS review.

I've been a big supporter of the DRS since it was introduced. I want it to help the umpires to get the big decisions — the ones that are clearly out or not out — correct. But when you get decisions like this one so wrong, that are so blatant, the video review system hasn't made any improvement at all. The onfield umpire made a mistake, and the third umpire repeated it. How has that improved the game? So furious were Cricket Australia that they took the unusual step of calling on the ICC for an explanation.

From a player's perspective, seeing this dismissal makes me realise why India don't want to use the DRS system.

But I had to push all of that out of my head. I was walking out to the centre. Chris Rogers and I had a quick word about it, but agreed that we had to put it behind us. We were two wickets down and in danger of wasting a great opportunity on a belter of a wicket.

As soon as I was in the middle, England brought on Broad and Anderson. The tactic to challenge me with short balls from their two main seam bowlers is par for the course now.

I defended Anderson, and then they gave Chris a single through cover off Broad to get me back on strike. Broad bowled a couple of bouncers to push me back, then some full outswingers. I got through that okay, and was pleased to be going to lunch to reset myself. I gave Chris a pat on the back for the way he'd played through that first session. He wanted to score more runs than he did in the first two Test matches, and today he backed himself and played with great intent. His 58th run today was his 20,000th in first-class cricket: a reminder of how much cricket experience he brings to the side.

Broad and Anderson continued after lunch, and I wasn't feeling all that fluent. Between balls, I practised hard on grooving my defensive shots and maintaining my balance. This was my first time in the middle since Lord's, and I needed to get my body moving in the direction I was hitting the ball.

The game went into a bit of a stop–start phase. Broad wouldn't complete an over until he had brought out the ground staff to work on the footholes he was making on and off the pitch. Then Chris, facing Swann, was distracted by someone in the pavilion behind the bowler's arm. It turned out to be Daniel Salpietro, who Chris knew. Once that had settled down, Chris came down the wicket to Swann and was hit on the pad. The umpire gave him out, and he asked me if I thought it was worth reviewing. Unfortunately, I agreed with the umpire this time. It might have been worth taking a chance on the review if we'd had two up our sleeve, but with only one, it looked too close to being out. The replays showed the ball going on to hit the stumps. I felt really bad for Chris, being only 16 runs from a Test century, but he'd done a great job for the team.

We had to survive another tense period after Steve Smith came in. He took a lot of balls to get off the mark, and while still on zero he played back to Swann and was hit on the pad. England appealed, Tony Hill gave him not out, and they called for a DRS review. It was extremely close yet again, but this time the decision went our way.

Swann was now coming around the wicket to me, with a leg slip in place, trying to get me the same way as Root had at Lord's. I went down the wicket to him when I felt I could drive straight or on the off side, but not when it was spinning past my pads. England left a big gap on the off side, with no fielders between slip and extra cover, to tempt me to cut against the spin. It was all about temptation, and me having the patience to resist it until I chose the right ball. From my end, that meant playing off the back foot to the ball on my leg stump, and either kicking it away or turning it around the corner for a single. When he gave it more air and it was on or around the off stump, I could come down the wicket and hit him over his head, pushing back the mid-off and mid-on, which Cook soon obliged by doing. That gave me the option of no-risk singles down the ground.

It was all very tactical. Smithy began to settle in and play some nice shots. Just before tea, Anderson hit him on the pads and England again reviewed the not-out decision. Again they were off the mark, and so they'd lost their second review. This came back to bite them a little later, when Smithy was absolutely plumb to Broad, the umpire gave him not out, and they had no comeback. There are so many ways the DRS can affect the game – Cook was now going through what I'd gone through in the first two Test matches, when you can lose your reviews very easily and then find yourself with no recourse when you get a shocker. The cricket community needs to think very hard about how to improve the system.

Root came on for a couple of overs after tea, but lightning didn't strike twice. Smithy and I battled on, urging each other to play straight and keep concentrating. Steve began to relax and play more of his natural game, while I struggled along, still feeling that I was short of my best rhythm. But the England bowlers, we could see, were growing tired and frustrated. Anderson's body language was looking a bit as if he thought this wasn't his day, and Broad kept stopping the game to repair the ground. The wicket was much harder than at Lord's, and Swann wasn't getting as much bite.

One of the most satisfying aspects of the partnership was that we didn't panic when they dried us up. When I got to 90, I spent about four or five overs when I didn't score a run. Smithy also went through lean patches. But the runs came again, and England misfielded, giving us more, as they grew tired. I drove Bresnan down the ground for four, but got through the rest of the 90s in singles. In these conditions, your potential worst enemy is yourself. The bowlers want you to get yourself out through impatience. It was hot and humid, as much a test for us as for them. I got to my hundred, but didn't celebrate with any huge theatrics. It felt almost like a 50 – the job was half done.

You can never relax for a moment. There's always a new threat. I played some streaky shots off Bresnan, who kept persisting, and then England took the second new ball. Anderson and Broad came back on for a last fling, but they bowled some loose ones, and Smithy and I found that the new ball was coming off the bat a heck of a lot faster. Broad soon seemed more interested in pitch repairs, again, and Anderson fell over after bowling a short one at me. He then bowled round the wicket, as if he couldn't handle the footholes at all, and was taken off. For us, that brief new-ball spell was a small victory. Seven overs into the second new ball, Swann was back on.

Importantly, we finished the day off. It's all very well to make some runs, but you can undo your good work if you lose wickets late in the afternoon. Smithy and I drove each other on to maintain concentration, and we completed the session together.

Once I got back to the hotel, I went straight to Alex for some physio. My back isn't 100 per cent, but if it's going to hurt, I'd rather it hurt after several hours of batting. It's no secret that I'm under pressure to lead from the front and make sure I'm scoring runs as a batsman. It's nice to get a few at last. I've been working so hard, and am happy to see it pay off.

But tomorrow's another day, and we need to be vigilant, or else what could be a commanding score will be just another mediocre one.

Friday 2 August. **Manchester.**

We're in a fantastic position after another good day, probably our best in the series. We have a lot of work to do tomorrow, but finally we're in the dominant role and have England on the defensive.

It was another warm day, and Smithy and I set out with great determination to keep the initiative and not give away our wickets. I had a slow start, playing out some maiden overs and not having much strike otherwise. Smithy was into his stride early, and I was very excited at the prospect of his First Test century. He's a much-improved batsman and he really deserved the three figures today, with a mix of stolid concentration and some beautiful shots, particularly through the off side.

Anderson and Broad came quite hard at us with the ball still new, but Broad was replaced by Bresnan after three overs. Anderson had a big appeal for LBW against Smithy turned down when his bowling hand brushed the bails on the way through and it was called a no-ball, a new law in operation for a few months. At any rate, it wasn't going to be out.

I was moving a bit more freely than yesterday, and took on Bresnan when he bowled some wide ones outside off. There was a short cover and a deepish cover. I drove him in the air between the two, and then straight above Swann's head at short cover. He got his hands to it and knocked it up, but it fell behind him and in front of the cover fielder further back. I was lucky, and knuckled down again to turn my hundred into a big one. Runs are always going to be easier now than later on, so I mustn't give it away when I'm settled in.

Smithy, meanwhile, was working his way towards his hundred. Swann came on from the Pavilion end, and tied him down with a few good balls. I'm sure Steve was starting to get nervous, because there's no other

THE THIRD TEST MATCH

explanation for what he did next, losing concentration and trying to hoist Swann into the new big red conference centre overlooking the ground from wide mid-on. The ball went straight up, and Smithy went off cursing himself. It's the third time he's been out close to a Test century. But I'm sure the youngster will get plenty more chances, the way he's going now.

An interesting moment ensued, when the crowd gave a prolonged boo for Davey Warner's entry. I had a good chat with him about the situation, and while he was nervous I'm sure he's the type of character who enjoys the confrontation. It's all part of the show. Joe Root wandered over and said, 'It's been a long two months, hasn't it?' which Davey found pretty funny.

I was getting some width from Bresnan. Three fours off three balls felt like a nice change, as it hadn't been an innings in which I'd ever scored freely for long.

Davey looked like he was getting into the mood too, coming down the wicket and cover-driving Swann nicely for four. But three balls later, the ball turned away from his forward defense and he nicked it. It bounced off Prior's thigh and popped gently to Trott at slip. At least, that's what everyone thought. But when Davey was given out, he came down the wicket to me and said, 'I don't think I hit it.'

I didn't say much. I thought he'd hit it, but he said he'd hit his pad. He was extremely confident he didn't hit it and wanted a review so I decided to back him, but sure enough the replay confirmed the big edge we'd all seen. Davey was booed off, but I doubt he would even have heard it. Having been booed myself, not only in a foreign country but by home crowds, I accept it as part of the game, and Davey is also one of those guys who is less likely to be bothered by it than stimulated by the challenge.

We had to push on, though, and Brad Haddin came out and played with fantastic intent from ball one. He lofted Swann over mid-wicket, then deposited Anderson over mid-on. When Hadds is playing his best cricket, this is the way he bats, and it's beautiful to watch.

The game moved into another of those phases where we were trying to press forward and England wanted to slow us down, which they attempted through tighter bowling and stopping the game for sawdust, pitch repairs, and so on. We expected a bit of gamesmanship, and generally laughed it off. Prior dropped Hadds off an inside edge, which helped our cause, and we were enjoying batting together.

There hadn't been too many demons in the pitch. It's very hard underneath. But now and then something is happening, some up-and-down bounce. Broad, to try a different tactic, came back on from the Statham end and bowled a lot of bouncers at me. Eventually one of them jagged back a mile, and I tried to weave out of the way. It followed me, got tangled up in my gloves and midriff, then dropped down onto the stumps.

THE THIRD TEST MATCH

So that was it. I'd have liked to keep going, but we were in a good position by now. I've been putting myself under some pressure to lead with a big score, so to make 187 is well and truly overdue.

Peter Siddle didn't last long, but Hadds and Mitchell Starc put on almost a century partnership in quick time – just what we needed to push past 500. Starcy showed today, for the first time in the series, what amazing hitting power he has – including one, down the wicket, that went straight into Hadds' body – and the potential that's there for him to become a genuine Test match all-rounder.

That partnership gave me the luxury of picking my time to declare. You have to think about the entire five-day length of the match at this point. In an ideal world, I'd have liked to rack up 650 runs in five sessions – and then bowl England out twice in a day! – but in reality, I had to consider the state of the wicket and our absolute need to win the Test match. We have to think about what's the best way to take 20 wickets, and my feeling is that we'll have to work very hard to get England out in their first innings, then bat again, and have a big crack at them in the fourth innings. So I preferred to get them in for their first innings sooner rather than later, and give our bowlers time to get two or three wickets before stumps today.

Which was pretty much how it panned out. I declared four overs after tea, at 7/527, rather than right on the tea break, just to limit the time England's openers had to get ready and to keep them guessing.

I gave our bowlers a bit of a taste to see how they'd go. Ryan Harris was straying onto Cook's pads a bit too often with the new ball, so I took him off after three overs to get Nathan Lyon into the game. He immediately had an effect — almost! His third ball got Cook's edge. It deviated onto Hadds' thigh and popped up in front of me. I could see it hanging there, but it was like everything went into slow motion. I couldn't get forward quickly enough, and the ball ended up landing probably halfway between Hadds and me, without having gone high enough for either of us to get to it. The sequence of edge, thigh, and lobbing up was almost identical to what happened to Davey Warner earlier today — except for the result. Cricket's a game of millimetres, that's for sure.

'Gazza' Lyon was putting a lot of revs on the ball and gave Cook some more anxious moments. There was a cut shot that screwed off the edge and fell just short of Warner at backward point. Starcy got one through Cook's defence and it fell close to his stumps, but not on them. This game can frustrate you sometimes. Watto had a chance at a run-out, but his throw missed. We really felt that the wicket was coming. Watto hit Cook in front, but the ball had pitched outside leg stump. I kept changing the bowlers in search of the man who was going to break through, and to keep the batsmen

THE THIRD TEST MATCH

from settling. Cook seemed to be unwell, too: he kept asking me if he could take a drink.

Peter Siddle, so reliable, was the bowler who did the trick. He bowled a beautiful-length ball to Joe Root, who nicked it to Hadds. Just classic fast–medium bowling.

Even though there was still half an hour to go until stumps, they sent Tim Bresnan out as night watchman. This was quite surprising. Bresnan's a good lower-order batsman, and had done the night watchman's job at Lord's, but this was quite a long time for him to survive.

It turned out that he wasn't in for long. Sidds bowled him a shortish ball, which he tried to pull. There was a noise as it went through and we all went up when Hadds caught it. The umpire gave it out, and I suspected that it would be referred. If the tables had been turned – if the initial decision was not out – I would not have asked for a referral. I just felt there was a chance it had hit his body and not his bat. So I was quite pleasantly surprised when, after a brief chat with Cook, Bresnan walked off. No arguments from me! But the replays did show that he'd most likely missed it. It's good to see that I'm not the only captain who gets these referrals wrong.

The night-watchman ploy had failed to come off. Trott, who looked in such good form in Nottingham and at Lord's, came in and started nervously. He would have run Cook out if Davey Warner's throw had been a few centimetres straighter. Then Trott got a healthy nick off Sidds, but it landed just short of me at second slip. So many 'nearlys'!

But we were still pretty happy when we came off for the night. We lead by nearly 500 runs and England have lost two wickets. Tomorrow's going to be hard. I can't see it being a day when we take a lot of wickets with catches at second and third slip. We'll have to bowl straight at the stumps and aim for LBWs and bowleds, with maybe some catches at short mid-wicket and short cover. When we produce chances, we *must* take them. Our bowlers are good enough to do that. As a team, we all have to be switched on, every ball.

The chances will come.

Saturday 3 August. Manchester.

I have mixed feelings about today. We did so many things well, and yet not quite as well as I'd hoped. The result is pretty good, to have got England seven wickets down with only 242 runs added in the day, but we didn't capitalise on opportunities we had.

The weather had cooled noticeably, and I spent most of the day in my sleeveless sweater. A fairly brisk breeze blew across the ground from east to west, helping the bowlers with any swing they might get. But the pitch was still very flat and playing well, and there was a lot less moisture in the atmosphere than in the first two Test matches.

THE THIRD TEST MATCH

We started with Peter Siddle and Ryan Harris, who had been the pick of the seamers yesterday afternoon. I set two short mid-wickets to Jonathan Trott, in case he got his balance too far across the stumps and lifted the shot to leg. For Cook, it was again the plan to tempt him in that fourth- and fifth-stump channel with the fuller balls.

Sidds had Cook playing and missing with just such a ball, and Rhino was tempting him into reaching for some drives outside his comfort zone. It's tense and fun at the same time, engaging in battle with good batsmen. When the rewards come, you're overjoyed. Cook played and missed with his pull shot, but it was Trott we got first, a ball from Rhino bouncing a little more than expected. The catch came to me at second slip where I had to lean forward to make sure it carried. A second-slip catch wasn't the central part of the plan, but there was still enough bounce to create a chance.

So, three down, seven to go. Kevin Pietersen came in and offered us a few opportunities early. He played and missed at several balls, and got off the mark with an inside edge past his leg stump. With good batsmen who start nervously, you always hope that you'll get them in the first few overs, and for us it wasn't to be. Pietersen survived that streaky period and I made a double change, bringing on Nathan Lyon and Mitchell Starc. Pietersen was still troubled, but got Starcy away with a couple of pull shots and gained some confidence from there.

Starcy has a knack for taking wickets, even if he's not as consistent as the other seamers. He broke through to pick up Cook, when Hadds took an absolute screamer down the leg side. I didn't feel that it was completely lucky to get the catch there. It's not one that you necessarily bowl for, but many batsmen are vulnerable if they move across too far and play a leg glance too finely. Still, it requires great wicketkeeping to finish the job, and Hadds is having a fine game. Taking that catch will have done a lot for his confidence.

Bell joined Pietersen, and continued his good form. Pietersen was always liable to take a risk if we dried him up, and he charged Watto once, edging the ball again a few centimetres past his leg stump. Starcy went around the wicket to Bell, to try to cramp him up on the off side, and just before lunch he played and missed at one – or so I thought. Hadds went up in a very loud appeal, while Starcy and I and everyone else did nothing. I was having a laugh with Hadds – 'Nice try, mate!' – but later there was word that Hot Spot might have shown a little tickle, so, as the wicketkeeper's always saying, maybe he does know best.

After lunch, Pietersen went after Nathan Lyon, lifting him for two sixes down the ground. He also gave chances though – again, he got a frustrating inside edge that could have gone into his stumps. And then he marched down the wicket at Watto, who was getting some reverse swing. The ball ducked back in and hit him on the pads. Watto went up, very confidently. When we talked to him, he said, 'It's got to be close.' But he wasn't super-insistent on referring. Hadds and I — and, for that matter, the umpire — believed Pietersen was so far down the wicket that the inswing would have taken the ball past leg stump.

So we didn't refer it — neither Hadds nor I thought it was worth it. A minute or so later, Hadds said, 'It was out.'

'Who said that?' I said.

He pointed up to the dressing room, where our analyst, Dene Hills, and Darren Lehmann were signalling with the finger that if we had referred it, Hawk-Eye would have shown that the ball was hitting middle and leg. I guess it was a mistake, but to be honest, if the same thing happened I would probably do the same thing. You just can't refer with any confidence when a batsman is that far down the track.

Watto took the disappointment without complaint, picked himself up and bowled a very good spell of reverse swing to Pietersen, challenging every part of his technique. We did dry him up, which we always feel is the first step to breaking his concentration. Meanwhile, though, Bell was able to score freely in his strong areas between mid-off and backward point, so we couldn't slow down the overall run rate enough to tighten the screws on either batsman. And sometimes the half-chances just don't go your way. There were quite a few of those in Pietersen's innings, and in the period I'm talking about, he went for a big off-drive that he snicked through a gap between second slip and gully for four. It could so easily have been a catch.

It took a very special piece of bowling to end that partnership, and Ryan came up with a perfect-length ball to Bell. It pitched around middle and hit the off bail. Bell did nothing wrong with his defensive shot – the ball was just at that precise length where the batsman couldn't confidently play forward or back. It took a terrific ball to straight-out beat a good batsman playing in the form of his life.

Pietersen, meanwhile, went on to make his century. We always thought we had a chance with him, though. After he got his hundred, Watto beat him outside the off stump with three balls in a row. It was *so* frustrating for all of us, and Watto's patience was tested. He has done a fantastic job with the ball, allowing me to rest the front-line seamers while he's tying down an end, but his figures haven't rewarded his effort yet.

On the other hand, Starcy has the knack for taking wickets. He was the one who got Bairstow, then finally got Pietersen for 113, sneaking one through for LBW. Pietersen talked with Matt Prior for a while before asking for a referral, which suggested that he wasn't too confident. There was some doubt over whether he'd nicked it, but the third umpire didn't have enough evidence to overturn the decision of the onfield umpire, and Pietersen was on his way.

THE THIRD TEST MATCH

There was always the chance of a collapse, but we couldn't quite pull it off. Overall the boys bowled well in patches, but I was disappointed that we didn't step on the throttle when we had the opportunity. The wicket was tough to score on because we had the ball reverse-swinging, and I thought Sidds, Rhino and Watto were all outstanding. Starcy got the three wickets, but didn't quite have the control he would have liked. Nathan Lyon bowled pretty well and I think he'll come into his own in the second innings.

In the morning, the plan is simple. We want to bowl well and take the last three wickets as soon as possible. England are still 30-odd runs from avoiding the follow-on, but my inclination is to have another bat, so that our bowlers can rest and the pitch can have a bit more wear and tear. When we do bat, we have to show intent and score quickly.

At some point tomorrow, I imagine I'll have to declare our second innings and set a target. It's going to be tricky to work out exactly when, and that's all going to depend on how well we bowl in the morning and then how fast we can score runs. There are forecasts of rain about, but there have been every day, and I can't think too much about that. Basically, we have to risk losing to try to win this Test match. That might mean a declaration that comes sooner rather than later, but at 0–2 down we have no choice. Sometimes in cricket you have to take that risk. We hope the game gives us the opportunity to win it.

That's all we ask for: the opportunity to see if we're good enough.

Sunday 4 August. Manchester.

I've had to sit for a while in my hotel room tonight, just calming myself down. The frustration really bubbled up today, and I had to keep telling myself that a captain mustn't lose control on the field. Privately, I can think my own thoughts. But as a leader, I have to set an example. The boys are really pulling together as a team, and keeping my composure is part of the leadership role I have to play. But that's not to say it's easy.

It's been one of those games where we got on top early, have remained on top, but have had to face a number of big and small obstacles. We're so desperate to win and stay in the fight for the Ashes that the battle against those obstacles is also a battle against our desperation. We want this thing so much.

England managed to stall us for an hour and a half this morning, their tail putting on 30 or 40 runs more than I was happy with. Prior, Broad and Swann also took up precious time by keeping us out in the field until half an hour before lunch. But still, we had plenty of time to set up a declaration and a fourth-innings push for victory.

While we were in the field, I asked David Warner

THE THIRD TEST MATCH

to open the batting with Chris Rogers. I wanted all the boys to play aggressively, and nobody has the capacity to do that better than Davey. Also, I wanted the three left-handers — Davey, Chris and Usman — in early and on their way before Swann came on. Obviously, the best outcome would have been for Chris and David to be still batting when Swann began bowling, but as the series has taken shape, we've concluded that it's particularly hard for left-handers to come in against the older ball and on the more worn pitch when Swann is turning the ball away from them. That meant Watto dropping down the order to number four, followed by myself and then Smithy. I also told Watto this while we were in the field, and he supported my reasoning.

Overall, I couldn't have been more pleased with the attitude and team spirit shown by the batting group. They all put team first, self second.

The English bowlers sent down a large proportion of short balls at Davey. I don't know if this was to probe a suspected weakness, or just to ginger him up and test him out after all the controversy. At any rate, he got into his stride very quickly and looked impressive. He missed one bouncer from Broad, and England referred it to the DRS when the umpire turned their appeal down. There was nothing to say he'd hit it, and he went on. The English took some time about getting back to business. Time meant as much to them as it did to us.

Chris kept the scoreboard ticking over, before

nicking Broad to slip. Usman also showed an unselfish, positive attitude. The pitch was starting to misbehave more often. Usman was beaten by one ball from Swann which bounced over the edge of his bat, over Prior, and even over Jonathan Trott at slip – and it hadn't even landed in the footmarks. There's definitely going to be something for Nathan Lyon to bowl into.

Davey eventually holed out to Joe Root at deep midwicket, but again, he was doing the right thing by the team. Then Watto and Usman pushed things along until Usman was bowled around his legs by Swann. I felt very relaxed when I went out – this was about as different a scenario as possible from two days ago. Watto looked in good touch. Then Bresnan bounced him, and Watto unfortunately steered it over the slips cordon to Kevin Pietersen, who was waiting at third man for the catch.

Smithy was in fine fettle again, picking up where he left off in the first innings. He was in a more attacking frame of mind, hitting two beautiful straight sixes, one off Bresnan and another off Swann. Speaking of Swann, a bizarre thing happened when he was bowling to me. He attempted what appeared to be a leg-spinner, but it came out of his hand like the famous balls John Howard bowled in Pakistan when he was prime minister. It landed halfway down the track and in my surprise, all I could do was follow it around on the leg side and paddle it away for a single. I guess David Warner sometimes bats right-handed, so Graeme Swann's allowed to try leg-spin.

THE THIRD TEST MATCH

The whole mood of batting was different from the first innings. After fighting for every run the other day, Smithy and I were now trying to hit the accelerator. Unfortunately, after nudging one fine of third man, Smithy, who's a very fast runner, turned and came back for a second without my hearing or seeing him. By the time I looked up, at the keeper's end after a comfortable single, Smithy was almost next to me. He turned and ran back, but didn't make it in time. It was the first run-out of the series for either side, which I guess is a measure of how grimly contested the Test matches have been. Both teams have been professional and careful with our running between wickets.

All along, I had to think about how long to go on batting. Ten minutes before tea, some light drizzle came down and the umpires took us off for an early break. This affected my thinking on a declaration. The early break meant that the last session would be something like 38 overs in length. We just felt that our bowlers, who had slogged away for 140 overs in ten hours of cricket to get England out, and had now only been resting for 30 overs, needed more of a break before they could make the most of the new ball. A 38-over session is a long one, and we thought that declaring at tea would also take the sting out of them for tomorrow. We want to make a really strong push for victory, but we need the bowlers to have the freshness and energy to do so.

For those reasons, our plan at tea was to bat for another 50 minutes before declaring and having some 20–25 overs to bowl tonight. Then the ball will still be relatively new when we restart tomorrow. The runs weren't so important. I am happy to give England a target they might think about chasing. So after tea, I just planned to bat for those 50 minutes.

The relations between the teams have been as competitive as you would expect in an Ashes series. But I don't think they've been poor, given the pressure everyone's under. England were doing all they could to slow the game down again, but nothing so extreme that they could get sanctioned for an over-rate violation. It's a matter of pushing the law to the limits, and Australian teams have done the same. Similarly, at one point I was pushing for a second run off Anderson, and when I turned to go, he had moved across the wicket into my path. I'm sure he didn't mean it, but he was right there and I went into him with my shoulder. It was an accident and some words were exchanged, but the senior players have been by and large keeping a lid on things. He looked like he was hurt, but I don't think he was.

Hadds got out playing a big shot for the team – more unselfish cricket – and Mitchell Starc and I were pushing the scoring along. The light was fading, but the floodlights were on and we were having no problem seeing the ball, even from the faster bowlers. Some of the England players were saying to the umpires that they were losing sight of the ball from the outfield, but this didn't concern me. The playing conditions say that the umpires can stop the game if safety is at risk. As batsmen, Starcy and I were feeling no risk at all. The outfielders aren't really relevant to that argument.

Starcy was out for 11, playing a big shot, but the first sign that the umpires were intending to move was when they asked Cook if he wanted to put his spinners on. He said no, of course. I thought this was a bit strange, as, being a batsman, I still felt no sense of danger. Then, suddenly, the umpires told me they were going to stop play.

I made my feelings clear, as coherently and respectfully as I was capable of doing in the frame of mind I was in. The issue here was that they had given Cook the option to bowl spin, but they hadn't given it to me. If they'd said, 'You can declare and bowl your spinners, but not your pacemen,' I would have seized that option – anything was preferable to stopping play. Nathan Lyon and Steve Smith would have happily taken a crack at the England openers. But as it panned out, there was consultation with the England captain and not the Australian captain, and this was what annoyed me.

So we've come off, extremely frustrated. It did rain, not too long afterwards, but that wasn't the point. When the umpires made their decision, we believed there were

32 overs remaining in the day. Now we've lost them, and only eight overs can be made up tomorrow.

Still, I have to forget that and carry on. We have every chance of winning, with plenty of runs on the board and 98 overs. There is an increasing amount of up-and-down bounce and certainly some spin in the pitch. I'm certain that if we get a full day's play, we will get ten wicket opportunities. If we can hang on to our catches and do everything right, we can win this Test match and the Ashes will be well and truly alive.

Monday 5 August. Manchester. Morning.

I didn't need to open my curtains and look out this morning to know that the sun wasn't out. There's a particular darkness to the Manchester sky when it's damp, and by the time I got up and had a look, it wasn't just cloudy but raining too.

Still, each day when I've looked at the local forecast on my iPhone, it has said it would be raining. And we've had almost four full days of cricket. It might rain this morning and then be finished by the time we start. We don't need a full day to bowl England out. I have every confidence in our bowlers and fielders – and the extra pressure of the scoreboard – that we can do it in two sessions.

THE THIRD TEST MATCH

Monday 5 August. **Manchester. Evening.**

There have been many frustrations on this tour, but none bigger than this. We really did have a strong position to win this match and stay in the battle to reclaim the Ashes. It wasn't inevitable that we'd win if we had enough time – but we thought we were good enough if we played our best. Having made such a fantastic start only sharpens the pain.

That rain I saw this morning left some moisture on the outfield, so when we got to Old Trafford, they had the Super Soppers and other equipment out to try to dry it up. It's amazing that in a summer when the pitches have been bone-dry to assist England's plans, it is rain that has foiled us in the end.

We got on an hour later than scheduled, at 11.30. We still felt that would leave us enough time if we got a good start. The game could go till 7.30 pm and we had been allocated a minimum of 98 overs.

An unusual aspect of the morning was that we were all out on the field, having a really good warm-up fielding, catching and bowling session, while the English were nowhere to be seen. Later we found out that they had been very slow turning up from their hotel, in the belief that the rain would have delayed the restart for much longer. Apparently their first few batsmen were there, but the rest of the team only turned up a short time before play began.

We were definitely ready. I'd declared, of course, and we started with Ryan Harris and Mitchell Starc taking the new ball. From the very beginning, the odd ball – maybe one every couple of overs – was behaving unpredictably. Some were taking off and flying through to the wicketkeeper at shoulder height, while others were keeping low from the same length. You couldn't tell, from looking at the pitch, what was causing this variation, but there were some cracks opening up.

Both new-ball bowlers were getting some movement in the air, too, and it wasn't long before Rhino bent one in late to hit Cook in front. We appealed very confidently, and the onfield umpire gave him out. Thinking he'd heard two noises, Cook referred it to the DRS. The replay showed that the toe of his bat had clipped his leg or foot, causing his confusion, but he was out and walking off before the decision even came through.

As we waited for Jonathan Trott to come out, I stood on the pitch, alone, for several minutes, thinking. I stood in the batsman's position on the crease, trying to work out exactly where to place the short fielders on the on side. We had to keep the initiative, and to follow our plan with Trott I had to be precise with the unorthodox field placements.

Starcy was bowling some excellent balls, as usual, including one skidder that very nearly trapped Joe Root in front. But he was also a trifle loose, allowing

THE THIRD TEST MATCH

the Englishmen to leave too many balls. Feeling that we had to keep them playing as often as possible, I brought Watto on from the Pavilion end for a couple of overs. He's been an invaluable bowler to have when we need to dry up the scoring, and I also think he's been very unlucky not to have taken more than one wicket in the series.

England were finding it extremely hard to score, and were 1/13 in the 11th over when we thought we had Trott. He shuffled forward to Ryan Harris and was hit on the pad. The umpire gave him not out, but I asked for a referral. This was a classic case of the benefit of the doubt going to the onfield umpire: to all eyes it looked like the ball was hitting the stumps, and Hawk-Eye had it hitting Trott's leg stump, but because there wasn't *enough* of the ball hitting *enough* of the stump, the third umpire ruled it umpire's call. That meant that if Tony Hill had given it out initially, his decision would have stood. And on top of that, Hawk-Eye itself has an acknowledged margin for error. We definitely felt that Trott was out, but the DRS ruling was quite consistent with the way it's been all series.

It didn't have too much of an effect on the game in the immediate sense. In Rhino's next over, Trott tickled one down the leg side for Hadds to take another good catch in what's been an outstanding match for him.

This brought Pietersen to the wicket, and I thought we might produce an error with spin, so I brought on

Nathan Lyon from the Pavilion end to replace Watto. But Pietersen was starting off in a more assured way than he had on Saturday. I also brought on Sidds to replace Rhino, who needed a rest after seven overs.

Sidds got the nick immediately, with the last ball of his first over. He got a beautiful delivery to rise on Joe Root and take the outside edge. The ball had remarkably good carry, not only to fly to my right at second slip, but to deceive me with how fast it was going. I got my hands out of position and the ball hit me on the wrist – and went down. I couldn't believe it. Again, I make no excuses. It was an unforgivable error at this stage of the game. As captain, I have to lead by example in catching as much as in batting. I was down on myself, and felt gutted for Sidds. I crossed paths with him at the end of the over and said, 'Sorry, mate.' There can't be many worse feelings on the cricket field than dropping a catch when the bowler works as hard for his wickets as Peter Siddle does.

At this stage, though, chances to take wickets were coming up regularly. Pietersen charged at Nathan Lyon, missed, and was lucky the ball turned into his pads. Next over, he played and nicked one off Sidds. There was a loud woody noise, and Hadds went straight up, though the bowler himself didn't react for a moment or two. Tony Hill gave Pietersen out. The batsman referred it, and lost. We had them three down, and they had no referrals left. The boys were getting very excited. It

Chris Rogers has a theory that English pound coins are heavier on the tails side, so I've called 'Heads' every match. At Trent Bridge and Lord's, it went against me. Here, at Old Trafford, it finally falls our way.

'Buck' Rogers batting beautifully at Old Trafford on the first day. He deserved hundred.

The English seamers bowled a lot of short balls at me. Here, at Old Trafford, I find a way to deal with one.

We get on the field and throw everything at the Englishmen. Here I'm asking for a referral for an appeal against Jonathan Trott. It counts for nothing: soon, the match will be abandoned. The Third Test is over.

Sidds lived up to his billing as the world's number five-ranked bowler with his energy and accuracy throughout the series. Here he celebrates a wicket with Hadds, day one of the Fourth Test, at Chester-le-Street.

Always something to think about. Despite the worry on Watto's face and mine, we're having a good opening day.

Ryan Pierse/Getty Images

Nathan Lyon, bowling beautifully on a pitch not offering much spin, appeals against Jonny Bairstow and gets his man, day one at Chester-le-Street.

At last! Five years after his Test debut, after scoring more than 20,000 first-class runs, after 30 minutes on 96, Chris Rogers has swept Graeme Swann away for four to bring up his maiden Test hundred. As a team, we could not have been happier.

Perfection, Ryan Harris-style. When a bowler of Rhino's class gets the ball in the right spot, no batsman can keep him out. Joe Root is his victim here at Chester-le-Street.

After so many injuries, Rhino got his rewards on this tour. Everyone converges on him after one of his seven second-innings wickets at Chester-le-Street.

Ian Bell on his way to his third hundred of the series, in the second innings at Chester-le-Street. He shows typical good style driving on the off-side.

The black clouds over Lumley Castle say something about our afternoon. I'm facing Graeme Swann. Things are about to get messy.

Straight after the drinks break, I'm bowled by Stuart Broad. If I had only stayed in for those five or six tough overs, I'm certain we would have won.

At the Fifth Test at The Oval, Watto went to number three in the order and made his highest Test score, an innings that gave a great boost to the entire squad.

He's been getting closer and closer, and now Steve Smith seizes his moment, driving Graeme Swann over the rope to bring up his first Test hundred. What few people outside our group know is how hard Smithy has worked to get to this point.

Smithy taking the plaudits after his innings at The Oval. I was particularly happy that he kept his head all the way to the end and stayed not out.

We started day five at The Oval looking to make something happen. Mitchell Starc helped things along by bowling Stuart Broad early.

Not quite finished! My back has stopped me from bowling as much as I'd have liked, but I send down two overs on the last day at The Oval. The batsmen aren't careless enough to give me a wicket, though.

It was the last ball of the series before we got our first run-out: Mitchell Starc throwing down the wicket to beat a diving Ian Bell. By by this stage we were playing under artificial light.

Aleem Dar reminding me to keep my distance as he and Kumar Dharmasena check the light meter, day five at The Oval. If I touched Aleem, I'd be looking at a few matches on the sidelines. Nathan Lyon, meanwhile, bites his tongue.

The end of the series. With four overs to go, we still thought we could take the last five English wickets. But the floodlights have come on, and the umpires are ordering us off.

When the reality hits us: England accepting the Ashes before a jubilant crowd.

You want to look away. It's devastating. But you need to use this moment to inspire you. Luckily for us, in three months we get a chance to turn this around

was typical of Sidds to bounce back so quickly after the disappointment of my dropped catch. He was all smiles, which made me feel a little better.

For the last over before lunch, I decided to have a bowl myself. The wicket was turning a bit, and that up-and-down bounce was continuing. As they hadn't seen me bowl all series, I hoped Root and Bell might be tempted into a mistake. I warmed up for several minutes, and felt confident that my back would stand up to it. As it turned out, nothing much happened in my over. Ian Bell slightly miscued a drive that went in the air close to Steve Smith at short cover, but nothing else of note. I was pleased to see I'm not completely past it as a bowler!

The weather, up to lunch, didn't look bad at all. The clouds were high and not looking too dark. But the forecasts were still gloomy, so it was disappointing to be going off for lunch when the weather was dry and the light was good. But the playing conditions are what they are, and they stipulated that lunch had to be taken at 1.00 pm, even though we had only bowled 20 overs in the first session.

During the break, a shower passed through. It left some moisture on the ground, delaying the restart by 20 minutes. When we got on again, Sidds was dangerous, sliding the first ball past Ian Bell's edge and then getting one to jump, hitting him on the thumb. Bell called for a trainer, and a few of England's support staff came out. Some of the boys thought this was overkill, but it was a sign of what we had to expect through the afternoon.

At any rate, it was all academic. The rain came down then, and despite a few breaks and moments of hope through the afternoon, we never got back on. The umpires came in and said to me, in front of most of the team, 'Even if the rain stops right now – and the radar indicates that it won't, there's plenty more coming – if we get back on the field, we will only have 12 overs of play.' In my mind, I was prepared to do anything – stay until midnight if need be – to get on the field, but I had to accept the reality the umpires were presenting. The best-case scenario was 12 overs, which was not enough. The match was abandoned, and the Ashes were retained by England, at 4.39 pm.

Everyone in the squad, from the players through to the support staff, is extremely disappointed and frustrated. Even the Doc, Peter Brukner, who's walking around in the pink blazer for being our 'one-percenters' champion in this match. All in all, we lost something like 110 overs from the match to rain, and it's hard to win a Test match when that happens on the last two days. That said, I'm happy with the position we were in and pleased that the Test match had reached the stage where only one team could have won it, and that was us. It wasn't inevitable, and we had seven more wickets to take, but I'm convinced that if not for the rain we would

THE THIRD TEST MATCH

be 1–2 down going to Durham, with all the momentum on our side.

But when you go 0–2 down in a series, you don't leave yourself with any margin for things like this to happen. I don't want to take anything away from England. They retained the Ashes by winning at Trent Bridge and Lord's. Our first-innings batting on both occasions was our major weakness, and I can offer no excuses there. Things definitely didn't go to plan.

Well, I certainly didn't expect to be writing this in my diary at this stage of the tour. But credit to the boys for showing some of their best work here in Manchester. At the post-match press conference, I was asked about whether this was a turning point for us and what it meant for the Ashes series in Australia this summer. I hope it means everything! But I can't think that far ahead. We have two hard Test matches ahead of us here. That's what I'm focusing on. We can take this momentum from Manchester and turn it into something really special, but on the other hand, if we execute badly, we can hand the initiative back to England.

That's the full reach of my horizon now, getting our team to perform consistently closer to its potential in the next three weeks.

The Aussie summer's still a long, long way off.

Third Test
1 August 2013. Old Trafford, Manchester.

Australia (first innings)

Batting		R	B	4	6	SR
SR Watson	c: Cook b: Bresnan	19	49	2	0	38.78
CJL Rogers	lbw: Swann	84	114	14	0	73.68
UT Khawaja	c: Prior b: Swann	1	19	0	0	5.26
MJ Clarke	b: Broad	187	314	23	0	59.55
SPD Smith	c: Bairstow b: Swann	89	196	8	0	45.41
DA Warner	c: Trott b: Swann	5	10	1	0	50.00
BJ Haddin	not out	65	99	6	0	65.66
PM Siddle	b: Swann	1	6	0	0	16.67
MA Starc	not out	66	71	9	0	92.96
RJ Harris						
NM Lyon						
	Extras (6lb, 2w, 2nb, 0b)	10				
	Total 7 Wkts, 146.0 Overs	527		3.61 Runs/Over		

Bowling	O	M	R	W	Econ	SR	Extras
JM Anderson	33.0	6	116	0	3.52		(1nb)
SCJ Broad	33.0	6	108	1	3.27	198.0	
TT Bresnan	32.0	6	114	1	3.56	192.0	(2w, 1nb)
GP Swann	43.0	2	159	5	3.70	51.6	
JE Root	4.0	0	18	0	4.50		
IJL Trott	1.0	0	6	0	6.00		

England (first innings)

Batting		R	B	4	6	SR
AN Cook	c: Haddin b: Starc	62	177	7	0	35.03
JE Root	c: Haddin b: Siddle	8	57	1	0	14.04
TT Bresnan	c: Haddin b: Siddle	1	15	0	0	6.67
IJL Trott	c: Clarke b: Harris	5	32	0	0	15.63
KP Pietersen	lbw: Starc	113	206	12	2	54.85
IR Bell	b: Harris	60	112	10	1	53.57
JM Bairstow	c: Watson b: Starc	22	51	3	0	43.14
MJ Prior	c: Warner b: Siddle	30	98	4	0	30.61
SCJ Broad	c: Haddin b: Lyon	32	66	7	0	48.48
GP Swann	c: Haddin b: Siddle	11	11	1	1	100.00
JM Anderson	not out	3	13	0	0	23.08
	Extras (17lb, 0w, 1nb, 3b)	21				
	Total 10 Wkts, 139.3 Overs	368		2.64 Runs/Over		

Bowling	O	M	R	W	Econ	SR	Extras
RJ Harris	31.0	9	82	2	2.65	93.0	
MA Starc	27.0	5	76	3	2.81	54.0	(1nb)
NM Lyon	35.0	12	95	1	2.71	210.0	
SR Watson	15.0	7	26	0	1.73		
PM Siddle	29.3	7	63	4	2.14	44.3	
SPD Smith	2.0	0	6	0	3.00		

Australia (second innings)

Batting		R	B	4	6	SR
CJL Rogers	c: Prior b: Broad	12	23	1	0	52.17
DA Warner	c: Root b: Bresnan	41	57	5	0	71.93
UT Khawaja	b: Swann	24	38	2	0	63.16
SR Watson	c: Pietersen b: Bresnan	18	24	1	0	75.00
MJ Clarke	not out	30	32	1	0	93.75
SPD Smith	run out (Prior)	19	19	0	2	100.00
BJ Haddin	c: Broad b: Anderson	8	9	1	0	88.89
MA Starc	c: Swann b: Anderson	11	11	1	0	100.00
RJ Harris	not out	0	3	0	0	0.00
PM Siddle						
NM Lyon						

	Extras	(2lb, 3w, 0nb, 4b)	9		
	Total	7 Wkts, 36.0 Overs	172	4.78 Runs/Over	

Bowling	O	M	R	W	Econ	SR	Extras
JM Anderson	8.0	0	37	2	4.63	24.0	(1w)
SCJ Broad	7.0	2	30	1	4.29	42.0	
GP Swann	15.0	0	74	1	4.93	90.0	
TT Bresnan	6.0	0	25	2	4.17	18.0	(2w)

England (second innings)

Batting		R	B	4	6	SR
AN Cook	lbw: Harris	0	9	0	0	0.00
JE Root	not out	13	57	1	0	22.81
IJL Trott	c: Haddin b: Harris	11	27	1	0	40.74
KP Pietersen	c: Haddin b: Siddle	8	16	1	0	50.00
IR Bell	not out	4	14	0	0	28.57
JM Bairstow						
MJ Prior						
TT Bresnan						
SCJ Broad						
GP Swann						
JM Anderson						

	Extras	(0lb, 1w, 0nb, 0b)	1		
	Total	3 Wkts, 20.3 Overs	37	1.80 Runs/Over	

Bowling	O	M	R	W	Econ	SR	Extras
RJ Harris	7.0	3	13	2	1.86	21.0	
MA Starc	4.0	2	6	0	1.50		(1w)
SR Watson	2.0	2	0	0	0.00		
NM Lyon	3.0	0	8	0	2.67		
PM Siddle	3.3	0	8	1	2.29	21.0	
MJ Clarke	1.0	0	2	0	2.00		

7

THE FOURTH TEST MATCH

Tuesday 6 August. Manchester to Durham.

Today's a quiet travel day for us. As I write this, we're on a five-hour bus ride from Manchester to Durham, right up in the north-east of the country. We don't actually stay or play in the town of Durham: we stay at Gateshead, which is the southern part of Newcastle, and we play at the town of Chester-le-Street, further south of Newcastle on the way to Durham. But it's known as the Durham Test match because Chester-le-Street is the ground of the Durham County Cricket Club. They're the newest club in the county championship, having been around for about 20 years, and this will be the first Ashes Test match at their ground. So we're going to be a part of history.

The boys are pretty sedate: sleeping, talking, watching movies, staring out the window. When we get there, we'll do our normal light recovery and rehab after a solid Test match.

There's some sunshine outside, which is nice, but the forecast for the next week up in the north-east isn't great.

Let's hope the weather defies the predictions, as usual!

Wednesday 7 August. Durham.

Our training session at Chester-le-Street was optional, but almost everyone in the squad came down. Guys were able to work on particular parts of their game or their fitness. For me, that meant no batting – I didn't pick up a cricket bat at all. With Alex, I had some treatment and did walking, running and cardio work. It's all a matter of flushing my legs out after spending a lot of time on the field at Old Trafford, as well as getting my mind right for what is a very quick turnaround between matches.

Like everyone else, I went through my rituals of unpacking my gear and laying it all out in the changing room. I went out to the middle and took a look at the wicket. It seems to be extremely dry . . . Have I said that before? It's very similar to what we've seen in all of the Test matches. There is some difference though: the cracks are fairly pronounced, and the plates of turf

THE FOURTH TEST MATCH

between the cracks are already moving about underfoot. It looks like a pitch that's ready to play on today, so let's see how it shapes up in a Test match lasting until a week from now. My guess, from how those plates are shifting, is that the ball will stay low. So on the batting side of it, that places an emphasis on good sound technique, playing very straight, being patient, and on the bowling side of it, attacking the stumps.

The other big story today is Hot Spot. I woke up this morning to see a 'major breaking news' story from Australia – that the inventor of the Hot Spot technology was planning to issue a statement alleging that England and Australian Test players were cheating, in effect, by putting silicon tape on the edges of their bats to somehow stop Hot Spot from showing up.

There have been some incidents where the technology has recorded a sound when a batsman's playing at the ball – a sound that you'd think can only come from the bat snicking the ball – even though the 'hot spot' isn't showing on the edge of the bat at all. So for some reason the technology isn't as accurate as hoped. Therefore the founder of Hot Spot is trying to come up with some reason why. The story said that he'd spoken to the ICC's Geoff Allardice, who was coming to England to talk to the teams and officials about it.

The whole thing caused a lot of laughter in our camp. We find it very funny. The player who seems to have been targeted by the allegations is Kevin Pietersen.

One point he made was why would he try to conceal the fact of the ball hitting the edge, when it could be just such an edge that saves him from an LBW decision? Of course, he said the story was a load of rubbish.

Which I agree with. Certainly in the Australian team, I know of no player to have spoken about ways of deceiving Hot Spot, and I know of no player who has done anything to deceive Hot Spot.

People draw a long bow sometimes. For example, the finger has been pointed at Extratec protective silicone tape, which is put around cricket bats to protect them. I've put Extratec on my bats since the age of 12. The reason? My parents couldn't afford new bats, so I had to do all I could to make my bat last as long as possible. Extratec costs five or ten dollars, and it protects a bat worth hundreds of dollars. For me now, putting on Extratec is just one of my lifelong habits. It's no different from wearing inner gloves while batting. When I was a kid, batting gloves cost fifty dollars and inners cost two or three dollars, so my parents would give me one pair of batting gloves and three pairs of inners, to make the expensive items last longer. I've stuck with them, not because I need to conserve gloves, but simply because it's what I feel comfortable with. Extratec is just the same. And I know I'm speaking on behalf of many players around the world.

For all the ludicrous side of the story, we were annoyed that the press ran with it and got it so wrong.

Fundamentally, it's an attack on the honesty of cricketers. Honesty and integrity have taken a few knocks in this series, and we're all a bit peeved that this adds to the atmosphere, when it has no basis in fact. To put it very simply, if Hot Spot isn't picking up nicks due to the presence of protective tape on the bats, then that's a problem with the technology. The approach should be to improve the technology, not blame the tape or cast doubts on the honesty of the batsmen.

Thursday 8 August. **Durham.**

We had another optional training session, where the batting group got through a fair bit of work, but some of the bowlers didn't come down, preferring to rest.

Late last night, we announced the squad of 12 for the Test match, and this morning we narrowed it down to 11 and settled on the batting order.

There are two main changes. In the bowling, we've decided to go with Jackson Bird ahead of Mitchell Starc. The selectors believe the conditions will suit Jackson. He's shown for a long time in first-class cricket that he's very good when the wicket doesn't offer a lot of movement. He's done extremely well in Hobart, playing for Tasmania, where the wicket can offer some assistance, but he's been equally effective away from home. On pitches that don't do as much, his record is very good. I think he'll come in and do very well. He's been outstanding in his two Test matches for Australia, taking wickets in Melbourne against Sri Lanka, and then being man of the match in the New Year's Test match in Sydney. He's probably unlucky not to have figured in more Test cricket, but he sustained a back injury and had to leave the Indian tour to recover, and since then he's been edged out by the fantastic form of Ryan Harris and Peter Siddle. This time he'll play alongside both of those guys, and we'll have an all right-arm attack.

In the batting line-up, we're doing a straight swap between David Warner and Shane Watson – Davey will open, and Watto will bat at number six. I like David opening: he's a very positive player at the top of the order and goes out there with great intent. He should combine very well with Chris Rogers. Those two at the top and Usman Khawaja at three means we're starting with our three left-handers. I expect them all to be facing Graeme Swann, but during the series we've seen how Swann relishes turning the ball away from left-handers when they're fresh at the wicket. It's very, very hard for them to start their innings while he's in full flight, turning the ball out of the footmarks.

I had a good chat about it with Shane at training. He's completely fine, and excited by the opportunity. He has often said he prefers to open, but he understands my reasoning. He also agrees that we can get more overs out of him if he's batting lower in the order. His overs are vital for the team, and he's been bowling very well. As a genuine all-rounder, it's hard for him to open the batting, and I look forward to being able to bowl him without having to think about resting him for his batting late in the English innings.

So here we are. We've tampered with this batting order a lot, but always in the interest of getting the right formula for the conditions and the attack we're facing. I hope we're getting closer to the right formula. We're excited and ready to play, and looking forward to playing a similar brand of cricket to what we produced in Manchester – only this time, with a Test match win to show for it.

Friday 9 August. **Durham.**

The day dawned beautiful and sunny, and as we made our way from Gateshead to Chester-le-Street, it looked like terrific weather for batting. As it turned out, we bowled, but had a fantastic day all the same. Our bowlers have done us proud yet again.

With the wicket looking very flat and dry, I would have loved to win the toss. It looks like it's going to be a very good batting wicket today and tomorrow. But I called wrongly again, and Alastair Cook elected to bat. On the upside for us, the weather was cool, with a nice breeze blowing across the ground to assist the swing bowlers. But it was clear, from looking at the pitch, that we would have to bowl a disciplined line and length and stick to our plans.

The English openers were not able to rotate the strike early, so Ryan Harris found himself bowling pretty much exclusively at Cook. Rhino really had his plans dialled in, and it was the fifth over of the game before Cook laid bat on ball. Up to then, Ryan had been probing and probing on that fifth-stump line, and Cook left a lot and played at a few.

At the other end, Jackson Bird slipped right back into the nice rhythm he has had in all of his games for Australia. He bowled at good pace to Joe Root and gave nothing away. We were probably a little bit too wide of the stumps for my liking, though. It looks like a new-ball wicket to me, so making the top-order batsmen play as often as possible is imperative. We weren't bad this morning, but could have tested them out just a bit more.

It was a slow start for England, and a relatively good one for us. I brought Watto on to replace Birdy, and eventually Root played forward to a good-length ball. We all heard a nick, but the umpire gave him not out. I wouldn't necessarily choose to risk losing a DRS referral so early in an innings, but Hadds was very confident and so was I, and sure enough the third umpire gave him out. It was Watto's second wicket for the series, which is a bit of a surprise given how well he has bowled for us.

Trott came in – a danger man for us, as we've found in the past, but he hasn't been making big scores in this series, despite looking in good touch. We placed a heavy leg-side field, sometimes with attacking catchers in unorthodox positions at short mid-wicket and leg slip, to dry up his strength in that area. When so much attention is focused on the on side, sometimes it's the other one that can be the surprise ball, and Rhino nearly got him when an outside edge flew towards the slips but landed just short of me at second. Then he chipped one off his pads, neatly – and frustratingly – bisecting the two short mid-wickets. It was a tense time.

Not long before lunch, I brought on Nathan Lyon from the Finchale end. The wicket didn't look like turning that early in the game, and it didn't, so Nathan had to adjust his line for very different conditions to those he bowled in just a few days ago in Manchester. He put in some tight balls to Trott, and then forced the error – Trott inside-edged one onto his pads, and it popped up square of the wicket. Usman Khawaja moved around and dived full-length to take a good catch.

It was great for 'Gazza' Lyon's confidence to take a wicket. As well as he bowled at Old Trafford, in the end it's wickets that bowlers are judged by, and judge themselves by. To remove such a key top-order batsman as Trott was a real shot in the arm for Nathan.

Kevin Pietersen came in, and made his intentions known straight-up. First ball, he charged Nathan and mis-hit a lofted on-drive. It lobbed just over wide mid-on. He kept coming at Nathan, and a couple of overs later I took him off, as much to disrupt Pietersen's plans and dry him up as anything else.

Watto played that role, and all the seamers were chiming in. Cook, at the other end, was surviving and accumulating, but that was about it. He played one nice cover drive for four off Watto, but the boundaries were few and far between. Pietersen called a very sharp run, and if Davey Warner's throw had hit the stumps Cook would have been out by several metres. The run rate was at or just below two an over. So even as the middle of the day approached, England were not really moving forward. We felt that if we took a couple of wickets, we could suddenly reverse the pressure and put it all on them, as a result of the small number of runs they had put on the board.

Pietersen was the one batsman who was going along fairly confidently, and after about half an hour I brought Nathan back on. England were 2/149, and we had to knuckle down to stop them turning a solid start into a big total.

Self-belief is everything in cricket, and Nathan has come back into the team with much more of it. Fifth ball, he slid one across Pietersen and drew the nick, which Hadds took safely. It was a big psychological breakthrough for Nathan to dismiss the guy who has tried so openly to dominate him – and it was a classic off-spinner's dismissal.

We had some momentum now, and Jackson Bird capitalised by bowling an absolute beauty at Cook. The

THE FOURTH TEST MATCH

left-hander had been leaving ball after ball – and we'd allowed him to – but now Birdy brought one back in and had him plumb LBW, not playing a shot. Great bowling. England would have been disappointed at tea, and even more so in the first over after the break, when Ian Bell also went after Nathan, charging down the wicket and only succeeding in lifting it straight of mid-off. Ryan Harris ran around to take a very good catch.

Nathan continued around the wicket, bowling an outstanding spell – nine overs, eleven runs, and two wickets. It was also good to see a bit of planning come off. We thought going around the wicket would be a good route of attack, given the ball wasn't spinning much. The angle brought into play the right-handers' outside edge if the ball didn't spin, and a potential catch in slips or behind. But if he could get the ball to straighten, he might get an LBW or a catch at bat-pad. That's all very well to say, but Nathan had to execute it, which he did. He's been working really hard in the nets, so it's good to see him get a result in line with that effort.

Bairstow and Prior went along steadily after tea, before Sidds got one to nip back in to Prior. The umpire gave him not out, and Sidds of course wanted a referral. Hadds and I were toing and froing for a few seconds, neither of us 100 per cent certain, but in the end it was one of those ones where we just said, 'We don't really know, but we have a gut feeling, so let's roll the dice.'

We had a good laugh when it came up our way. The overturning of the decision was due reward for another typically stout effort from Sidds. He's earned a great deal of respect in England on this tour.

I brought Nathan back on, and he was going so well that I delayed taking the second new ball by four overs. Bairstow tried to sweep him across the line from around the wicket, a risky shot, and was LBW. That gave Gazza a well-deserved four-for. Broad and Swann were caught off the seamers trying to play big shots, and while we'd have liked to finish the England innings off today, a few late blows by Anderson couldn't take the shine off a performance that continued the upswing we started in Manchester.

We're still far from completely satisfied, though. After play Darren talked to the boys about execution with the new balls, both first and second, and we recognise a need to make the most of it in the second innings, making the batsmen play as much as possible.

Overall, a very pleasing day. Tomorrow, the battle between our top order and the new ball will be vital. We absolutely must put up a good first-innings score. If we bat like we did in Manchester, we'll be in a good position to win this Test match.

If cricket was the only important thing in life, that would have been it for today. But I wanted to get back to our hotel overlooking the River Tyne to celebrate one of the biggest days of the year: my beautiful wife's birthday. Kyly got a few presents from the partners who are still travelling with the team, and her family sent her a gift from Australia. She had a nice day out, and we've just had a nice dinner together. I can't emphasise enough how great it is having her on tour. When I get back to the hotel each night she takes my mind off cricket, which, as any sportsman knows, is essential to keeping your mind fresh. Not only that, of course: this has been a special time for the both of us to spend together.

Saturday 10 August. **Durham.**

Today was a highlight of the tour for two teammates. Our position in the game is promising if not secure, but it's one of those days when we are celebrating each other's success.

The weather up in the north changes fast, and so do conditions, as we found out this morning. With a bit more cloud cover, combined with the effects of yesterday's play, there was a considerable amount of swing and seam movement. We discovered this early, in the couple of overs we bowled before we finished England's innings: our quicks were getting more out of the conditions than they had yesterday. Jackson Bird got plenty of zip and swing, hitting James Anderson on the helmet before bowling him with a big inswinger to the left-hander.

This lateral movement was confirmed when we went out to bat. It looks like a new-ball pitch, and so it proved. Chris Rogers and David Warner had to be very careful. From the first over, Chris was having to control a ball coming off the edge, using soft hands and playing late to keep it down.

We were just showing signs of comfort, with the boys picking off a two, a three, a two and another three off four consecutive balls from Broad. That's a lot of running. Davey was facing the last ball of the over when he tried to let it go, but it was pitched on a perfect top-of-off length and it clipped off his bails. Usman Khawaja got a nick two overs later, and I was out there with Bucky.

It was quite cool and grey now, and I was wearing my vest. I was out there for a little while before I had to face a ball. Chris was facing Anderson from the Lumley end, and I was busy running – and almost slipping over – while he scored a two, a couple of fours, and a single before I had to take guard the first time.

My first runs came off the inside edge, and I had to stop the game because of some movement behind the bowler at the Finchale end. Chester-le-Street is another ground where seating is allowed below the sight screen, and throughout the series players have asked the stewards to try to minimise the distraction caused by people moving. I was just trying to get through what was a tough period in unfamiliar conditions, but the action started happening at the other end.

THE FOURTH TEST MATCH

Broad was bowling to Chris, and hit him in front of the stumps with a ball that appeared to pitch outside the line of the leg stump. Umpire Tony Hill turned down their appeal, and Cook decided to refer it. As Chris and I expected, the video showed that it was not out. That meant England were down to one more unsuccessful referral.

Chris hit a four off the next ball, a no-ball. Then, the last ball of Broad's over went through Chris and was caught behind. The English appealed, having heard a noise, and this time Hill raised his finger.

It didn't take more than a few seconds for Chris and I to agree to review it. Chris asked if umpire Hill had given him out caught or LBW, and Tony said caught. This would prove important. Chris was certain the ball had hit his leg, not his bat, and from where I was standing I thought that could well have been the case.

The replays showed pretty clearly that Chris was right – the ball had missed his bat and clipped his thigh as it went through to the keeper.

But the drama didn't end there. Hawk-Eye was showing that the ball, even though it hadn't hit his bat, would have grazed the stumps. If it was an LBW decision, the DRS was saying it was umpire's call.

Thinking umpire's call meant that Tony Hill's decision would be upheld, the English players started celebrating. But they had it wrong. If it was umpire's call on the LBW, Chris was not out. Tony Hill hadn't given him out LBW. So, correctly, Tony changed his decision and said Chris was not out.

This set the English players off. They were questioning the umpire about why Chris wasn't out, when he had given him out and the DRS said it was umpire's call. I stood by and listened as Tony explained the situation. It was clear that they didn't know the rule. It was all a lot of confusion and discussion for what was, in the end, the correct result, I felt. Chris hadn't hit the ball, so he wasn't out caught. And it couldn't be given out LBW. So, what it was, after all that, was a dot ball.

After drinks, Tim Bresnan replaced Anderson, but it was Broad who was giving me problems, bowling a very good length from the Finchale end and getting just enough lateral movement to be a handful. He hit me on the pad, and they went up for an appeal, but it was going down the leg side. Then he beat me with a jaffa that passed close to my off stump. I had to focus here.

Chris was settling in well, and needed me to support him. He took two fours off Bresnan's next over. As I was settling in to face Broad, an elderly lady was moving around behind him. I motioned to have her sit down, and in the end I made the mistake of not backing away and starting my preparation from the beginning, instead just giving a wave while I was in my stance. It was poor mental application, in retrospect. Broad came in and bowled a wide ball. I went for a drive, and edged it high to first slip. Cook took the catch, and I was out for six.

THE FOURTH TEST MATCH

I was cursing myself for giving my wicket away so early, but meanwhile the game was going on. Steve Smith went out there and played very confidently from the start, middling his defensive shots and leaving the ball well. By the time I'd packed up and come out to the balcony to watch, Smithy was in full flight. Anderson came on to replace Broad, and Smithy put away a leg-stump half-volley for a boundary, suggesting he was carrying on his form from Old Trafford.

When they came in for lunch, I was feeling brighter about things. Chris was looking particularly solid, and we had high hopes for a big innings from Smithy.

Unfortunately, he was out to a regulation nick to Bresnan just after the resumption. This brought Watto to the wicket. At 4/76, he was facing a ball not much older than when he'd been opening. So at least he was used to this – and he had, at the other end, the bloke he'd opened with in the first three Test matches.

It's a wicket that you're never really 'in' on, never more so than today. Chris and Watto went through a very tough period in the hour after lunch. The ball went past the bat a fair bit, and they needed the rub of the green. Shane hit one very hard and straight that Bresnan got a hand to, and then Chris, after having a struggle against Broad, nicked one low to second slip, where Swann put it down. They were both extremely difficult chances, so while you could say the batsmen were lucky, you could also say they would have been unlucky to be dismissed. The single that Chris took from that dropped chance brought up his 50, but he didn't celebrate much, giving the impression that he was set on bigger things.

Towards drinks, the ball began to soften and the sideways movement eased off. Watto had toughed out a very hard period, but began to open out now, hitting three fours just before the break. When it came we were 4/119, exactly halfway to England's score.

Jonathan Trott came on for a few overs of medium pace, not a bad move considering the conditions. Swann had a bandage on his third finger after hurting it trying to catch Chris at slip, and wasn't doing much bowling. But after Watto had hit Trott for a couple of boundaries, Swann came on from the Finchale end. Now came a different kind of test. After the swing and seam earlier, how much turn would there be?

Watto and Chris dealt with it maturely – I'd even say, magnificently. They were building what I believe has been the best partnership by either side in the series so far. To hold their nerve and get through so much pressure, both from the match situation and from the way the ball was ducking about, was just brilliant to watch. The conditions wouldn't allow them to dominate, but they were asserting control over the bowling.

After passing his half-century, Watto unfurled some superb shots. There was one straight drive off Anderson that he hit so hard, the English gave the ball to the umpire

THE FOURTH TEST MATCH

when they'd fetched it from the boundary, thinking it must have been knocked out of shape. Watto was coping with everything they threw at him, and was batting with fantastic determination. Chris, meanwhile, was picking his areas to score, and doing it well. He peeled off a beautiful cover drive from Swann to go to 96. Just one more boundary! But then he tried to turn one off his legs and only managed to pop it up into the infield on the on side. It landed between fielders. On the balcony, with Davey Warner beside me, I let my head fall into my hands. It was so tense, and we wanted this for our teammate so much!

By drinks in the last session, Chris was still 96 and Watto was 68. We were 4/205 and getting very close to overhauling England's score. If only we could hold it together, we might build a decent lead and apply some scoreboard pressure from our side.

Unfortunately, the partnership wasn't to continue for much longer. The clouds were closing in and the light was failing. Chris blocked out a maiden from Swann – we were very nervous, but I can't say how he was. Then Broad came on from the Lumley end, and the last ball of his first over back was a rubbish ball down the leg side. Watto was agonisingly unlucky to get a slight touch to it. He isn't the first batsman in this series to get out caught down the leg side, but I don't think there's been a less fortunate one. He deserved a hundred. His score of 68 doesn't do justice to a great innings, that's for sure.

I know, having been there myself, that it must have been unsettling for Chris to lose his long-term partner so close to reaching his century. He then went through another tough period that had us all in agonies. Swann bowled exceptionally well and tied him down. We were praying that he'd get a full toss to put away, or be able to get up the other end and get something easier to score off from the faster bowlers. Hadds, taking on Broad, turned one behind square, and we thought Chris might get up that end – but they took a two, leaving Chris facing Swann again.

He's scored something like 60 first-class centuries, but later he said that none of them was any kind of preparation for the pressure of doing it in an Ashes Test match that was right on the line. Still, I reckon I was more nervous watching than he was out in the middle. Finally, after half an hour on 96, he took a small risk against Swann by going down and sweeping. He got it away through the gap at square leg, and it was done – he had his century. In three weeks, he'll be 36 years old. It's an amazing achievement. I guess the moral of the story is, never give up!

A very short time later, the umpires decided enough was enough, and stopped the game for bad light. That gives an idea of how difficult the conditions were for the batsmen at the end. Hadds was having to play strictly straight, digging out balls that were keeping low, putting every ounce of concentration into the task.

When they came in, the boys were extremely excited for Bucky. We'd all been outside, packing the balcony, when he made his hundred, and we were still out there to cheer him and Hadds in. What a day. He'll cherish it for the rest of his life.

While still at the ground, we had a beer or a soft drink with Chris. It's a tradition in the team that we do this to celebrate a player's success when he scores a hundred or takes five wickets in an innings. I just felt so pleased for him, to have this against his name after so many years when he thought he might not get back into the Test team. It was a great lesson in persistence for everyone.

Tomorrow's another day, though. The weather changes quickly here, but we're hoping for some sunshine. The new ball is due more or less immediately, and we're looking to Chris and Brad to continue where they left off and build us a score somewhere beyond 300. Then we'll have a chance to turn the screws.

Sunday 11 August. **Durham.**

Our first objective for the day was to build a lead. I was hoping for something in the region of 70–100 runs. But it went wrong pretty quickly. Graeme Swann bowled an outstanding spell with the old ball, and turned one sharply in to Hadds in the second over of the day. Hadds had it referred to the DRS, but the ball was going to hit leg stump. It was a big wicket for England.

Worse was to follow when we lost the second of our remaining senior batsmen. Chris Rogers played forward to Swann. The ball popped up off his thigh, and Matt Prior ran around from behind the stumps, dived towards short leg, and caught the ball in his outstretched glove. The English appealed, but Tony Hill gave Chris not out. Prior was adamant and they quickly referred it. Hot Spot showed a very fine mark on Chris' left glove, and the replays revealed a small deviation in flight. So England got their reward, and the second rock in the foundation of our batting plan for the morning was gone.

Yet again, we needed runs from our tail-enders. Surprisingly, Cook took the new ball when Swann was bowling so well. But it has been a new-ball wicket, and at first the move paid off, when Sidds nicked Anderson. We were eight down, with barely a lead to show for it, and were losing wickets in clumps again.

Fortunately, Ryan Harris, who has been such a champion for us on this tour in every way, connected with the new ball and hit 28 runs off 33 balls. Those were incredibly valuable runs, and may become more so as the match goes on. I was really impressed with how freely he played, the sign of a clear mind and a bloke who would do anything for his team.

He was out in somewhat comical fashion. Broad had him absolutely plumb LBW, but it was given not out by the onfield umpire. The English referred it to the DRS. While they were waiting, the English blokes asked Ryan if he'd hit it. He said he hadn't, and couldn't understand why it hadn't been given out, though there were two noises – it was the ball hitting his front pad and his back pad. Anyway, as soon as they saw the replay on the big screen, the players, English and Australian, walked off. They were halfway to the pavilion when umpire Tony Hill received the information and raised his finger – on an empty pitch.

Ryan and Jackson Bird were straight back out there with the new ball. We had to make this period count. Our lead was 32 – less than I'd hoped for, but more than looked possible before the partnership between Bucky and Watto.

Immediately, there was variable bounce. Birdy got one to shoot on Cook, and Root nicked him just short of me at second slip. Unlike two days ago, the boys were really attacking the stumps with the first new ball and were forcing the English openers to play. Eventually Rhino bowled an absolute pearler to Root, the perfect example of 'top of off'. His strength as a bowler is sometimes no more complicated than that: he puts more balls in that area, so he's giving himself a chance to create danger with the natural variation provided by the wicket. It's simple to plan, but requires great concentration, skill and preparation to pull it off consistently.

He was bowling a brilliant spell. When Jonathan Trott came in, I placed Usman Khawaja at a widish leg slip – probably the equivalent to about second or third slip. Immediately, Trott turned one at catchable height down the leg side, but it went between Usman and Hadds. I went over to Usman to size up the angle, thought about it for a minute, and moved him finer.

After lunch, Rhino adapted his plan to Cook, bowling that tempting full length outside off stump. Soon enough, Cook went for the drive and nicked it. Both openers gone, and England still behind us.

From the Finchale end, Jackson Bird was getting a few to shoot low. Watto came on and he was also getting the variable bounce, which was more pronounced from that end. It was Rhino, though, from the Lumley end who was doing the damage. He saved up his bouncer against Trott for just the right moment, and caught him out of position, fending and gloving the ball through. It looked like it was going over Hadds. I felt myself go up onto my toes as I watched. Almost in slow motion, Hadds leaped up and took a brilliant overhead wicketkeeper's catch, one-handed.

This brought out Bell to join Pietersen. We've had England three wickets down for not many on plenty of occasions in this series, and haven't been able to drive the advantage home. That's often been due to Bell, who has batted as well this summer as I've ever seen him. There's nothing that I can detect that's different about his game. He's always been technically very orthodox. It's probably been mentally where he's matured and just become a more calm, confident individual.

The wicket was slowing down again, after gaining a bit of zip through yesterday's play. We were testing Pietersen and Bell with a mix of tactics. Sidds dropped short a few times to Pietersen, but the batsman got the better of that battle. Soon I had to worry about the runs accumulating. This is one of the trickier challenges for a captain: when you know you need wickets, when wickets are the best way of stemming the flow or runs, but when you also can't afford to let the runs get away from you. I dropped a third man into place for Bell; I don't usually like a third man, as it's such a defensive position, but he's scored so many runs through that region with his late cut that I had to try to turn his fours into ones.

I brought Nathan Lyon on, and once again he bowled very tightly from around the wicket to the right-handers. Pietersen was clearly trying to make adjustments after his first-innings dismissal, and wasn't taking Nathan on as brazenly as he did the other day here and at Old Trafford.

Meanwhile, I was suffering from a headache, and asked Alex Kountouris to come on with a drink of water and some pain relief.

After tea, we lost our way a little. It was quite cold and I was one of several players to be wearing two sweaters.

This made it a danger period for the bowlers, injury-wise. Rhino got Bell to inside-edge one, but it flew just clear of Hadds' dive. The boys kept trying, but the strain was beginning to take its toll. Watto, who has bowled so tirelessly for us throughout this series, suddenly pulled up after delivering a ball and said he was feeling a twinge in his groin. When he went off, it made it that much more important for all of our bowlers to maintain discipline. Jackson Bird finished Watto's over, and immediately hit Pietersen in front. We appealed, were turned down, and referred – but lost the referral when we got it wrong. Eventually, Pietersen went forward to Nathan Lyon and made the crucial error. On Friday, he tried to hit Nathan through cover and nicked one with an open face. Today, he tried to play the same ball onto the leg side, closed the face, and chipped a leading edge to short cover. For Nathan, it was extremely satisfying.

After that, though, Bell continued defying us. Birdy and Nathan bowled some good balls, and Sidds kept on trying, but the game felt like it was slipping away. Bell was playing patiently, using the pace of the ball, and at times we gave him too much width. The wicket was playing well, not offering as much movement as yesterday. What we really needed was to get a couple of wickets in a row, to establish momentum, but all day we hadn't been able to achieve this.

We kept plugging away, nobody more so than big Rhino. Jonny Bairstow put him away for a couple of fours, and Rhino had an idea that he might disrupt Bairstow's footwork by coming around the wicket and bowling short. He sent down three perfectly targeted bouncers, all of which Bairstow had to play. Then Bell got on strike, and Rhino set him on his backside. To bowl with that amount of energy and intent, at this stage of the day and the Test match – all you can do is sit back and admire such a bowler, and be glad he's on your side.

Nathan kept tying them down from his end, and eventually got another reward, Bairstow edging to Hadds.

Bell kept going, though. He's been such a thorn in our side in this series. Not many people have ever scored three centuries in an Ashes series, and he's a player who's earned our respect over the years. It's a game of centimetres, though, and we *nearly* had him for 97. I stationed myself at about a third-slip position, and Jackson Bird bowled a beautiful ball, a slow off-cutter that jumped a bit. Bell took the bait and cut at it. It came off the edge, at head height . . . and just out of my reach, to my left-hand side. So close.

He got his hundred, and when we came off the field we all shook his hand. It's an impressive achievement. Then we all gathered around and congratulated each other on another hard-fought day.

We're disappointed to lose Watto from the bowling attack for this match, and we'll have to wait and see how he shapes up for The Oval Test match. The important thing right now is to bowl well in the morning to keep England's lead to a minimum, and then bat extremely well to chase whatever's required to win this Test match.

Monday 12 August. Durham.

I am struggling to come up with the words to explain the disappointment I'm feeling now. The Test match is over. What a day. I'm in shock, to be honest. I don't know what else to say. Over the coming days, I will try to find consolation and maybe inspiration from those who are closest to me, but right at this moment there is only devastation. The worst thing is that we know we're good enough to win these matches but can't seem to find a way to do so.

This morning, it was another typical Durham day, with all four seasons within every hour. It can be sunny one minute, then cloud over and rain the next; cold enough to wear two sweaters, and then a nice burst of sunshine that has us down to short sleeves. One thing we knew was that the wicket was not deteriorating as much as expected, so whatever we had to chase in the fourth innings, we would have plenty of opportunity.

We had a few overs with the old ball to start off, and I trusted Nathan Lyon and Peter Siddle to bowl tightly to Bell and Bresnan, the night watchman. When the new ball came, Ryan Harris and Jackson Bird made it a new game. Almost immediately, Birdy had Bresnan padding up to one that nipped back, and it looked LBW to us. The umpire, Aleem Dar, gave it not out, so we referred. It was another case that made us scratch our heads: the ball tracker said it was hitting leg stump, but not enough of leg stump to make it definitive, so it went back to umpire's call. Considering what happened later in the day, it feels gut-wrenching to know that Bresnan, who went on to score a few more vital runs, was able to escape when he was padding up to a ball that definitely would have hit the stumps.

Ryan Harris was a titan again, putting the ball in the places where it could be most dangerous. He's bowled exceptionally well in three Test matches now. He got one off a good length to shoot on Bell, and bowled him. Next ball, to the new man Matt Prior, was pitched in about the same spot, but this one jumped off a length and the batsman could only parry it down into his stumps. It was great bowling, yet again.

Stuart Broad survived the hat-trick ball – a good one just outside off stump – but in his next over Ryan got him with a steeply rising bouncer that he gloved away for the catch.

We wanted to finish them off there and then, but yet again the tail-enders were able to skim off some cheap runs. Bresnan and Swann were pretty much backing away and slogging, but they got away with a few fours and put on nearly 50 runs for the ninth wicket before

Rhino dismissed Bresnan. They were runs we could have done without conceding. Our bowlers got a bit frustrated and tried to bowl too short, and the batsmen were lucky to connect with a few. It was in this situation that I have become used to throwing the ball to Watto. But he wasn't available. The good news was that he was able to field, however, so it meant he should be eligible to bat in his usual position, if needed, later in the game.

By and large we have caught very well, with Hadds leading the way. I don't think we've let ourselves down with our fielding. Unfortunately Smithy grassed a boundary catch off Swann towards the end, but it didn't cost us many runs. I was happy that Nathan Lyon, the unlucky bowler in that instance, was the one who ended up taking Bresnan's wicket.

So we had precisely 299 runs to win — just a few less than at Trent Bridge. We would have liked to be chasing a smaller target, but I can't take anything away from our bowlers. On our side was that this wicket was holding up better, and there was nowhere near as much reverse swing going on. We had ample time — five sessions in all — so there was no pressure in that regard. The pitch has been difficult for the batsmen all match, but we would have no excuses if we didn't make it.

Chris Rogers and David Warner had a short session of batting before lunch, and got through it comfortably. The new ball wasn't veering about as much as it had on Saturday, and encouragingly both of the boys were looking neat and tidy in their defensive play. Anderson had a big LBW shout against Chris, but it was given not out, and surprisingly England referred it. Bearing out the umpire's decision, the ball was shown to have pitched several centimetres outside Chris' leg stump. So England now had only one unsuccessful referral to the DRS left.

We were halfway into our lunch break when a heavy rain shower swept in. This didn't concern me, as we had so much time up our sleeve. But if we did build up some momentum through the afternoon, it would be an added challenge to have to come off and break concentration for rain delays. When a bowling team is feeling the pressure, an interruption and a chance to rest up and reboot in the changing rooms can give them just what they need.

The resumption was delayed by an hour. When they went back out, Chris and David dug in and tried to keep out the good balls. Broad started with a very good over to Chris, bowling one that hit him on the pads, one that went past his outside edge, and one that popped up off a leading edge and fell just short of the diving bowler. But the good thing about an experienced batsman like Chris is that he can count that as a victory: dangerous balls have come and gone, and he's still there. Rather than feeling that he's being dominated, he can move on to the next ball and feel confident that he's survived. Chris did just that, and tucked away some singles before putting

Broad away with a beautiful drive through wide mid-on, one of the best shots of the match.

Davey, meanwhile, was going along extremely well. Davey was waiting for the ball to come under his nose and punching it away, particularly through the arc between cover and mid-off. We've seen a lot of him batting positively at the top of the order in the last couple of years, but at his best he combines that intent with a very sound defensive technique.

When Chris was on 14, he had a scare very similar to the one he survived when I was with him on Saturday. A ball from Anderson went through him, hit something, and England were given the decision. Chris shook his head and quickly referred it to the DRS. For all the issues around the system, it can be credited with overturning quite a few incorrect onfield decisions. This time, just like in the first innings, the replays showed the ball to have hit Chris' body, not his bat, and he was allowed to stay out there.

Soon after, he edged Bresnan into the slips cordon and Graeme Swann dropped it, diving to his right. It was uncanny, how these two let-offs followed the same course as in the first innings. Was history repeating for Chris? I certainly hoped so.

These nervous moments became fewer as the partnership went on. Chris and David ran aggressively between wickets and put the pressure back on the fielding team. As the runs started to accumulate, we felt more

THE FOURTH TEST MATCH

and more confident that we could win this Test match. Swann came on, and three balls into his spell Davey lofted him over extra cover for six. When I thought back to Davey batting at number six in the first innings at Old Trafford, it struck me what a difference there is between coming in and facing Swann straight-up, and first facing him when you've been batting for an hour and are seeing the ball well.

Chris was also getting Swann away for runs when he overpitched, and the boys went to the mid-afternoon drinks break at no wicket for 80 – still a long way from home, but in a very promising position.

One of the best things about Davey's batting was how patient he was. Around this point, after motoring along at a run a ball, he went through a half-hour period when he hardly scored a run. Swann was bowling a full length, with a long-off out for protection, and Davey couldn't penetrate the off side field. What was most encouraging was that he didn't lose patience or play a bad shot. He just stuck with his plans and waited. Soon enough, he got one through the off side for a boundary. On strike to Broad, he upper-cut a short one safely over the slips cordon for four, and the runs began to flow again. He brought up his 50 with a back-foot punch through cover point off Bresnan. We were past the hundred – a third of the way to victory – with all ten wickets intact.

Chris looked like he was headed to another half-century too. Swann bowled a half-tracker which he swung away for four to reach 49. It was terrific to see him following up his century with more outstanding batting. But there's always the threat of a good ball around the corner with Swann, and the next delivery was just that, pitched up and turning away, and Chris edged it to slip.

At 1/109, we were still on track, however. Usman Khawaja looked very calm, tucking his first ball off his hip for two, and he and Davey enjoy batting together. Usman straight-drove a full toss from Swann very nicely for four, and the boys came in to tea with the score on 120 – very promising indeed.

There was nothing special or unusual in the conversation or planning. We came here today to win the Test match. At tea, as far as we were concerned, we were methodically going about winning it.

England began the last session with Swann from the Finchale end and Anderson from the Lumley end. Our boys resumed nicely. Usman got some runs away off Anderson, and Davey played a nice late cut off Swann, timing it well and bringing up a boundary behind point. It was against the run of play, then, when Usman missed a full-pitched ball from Swann, was hit on the pad, and was out LBW for 21.

My first concern, when I walked out to join Davey, was to keep the momentum going. The boys had played so positively, establishing a really good mood around the run chase, that the project was simple: keep it going.

THE FOURTH TEST MATCH

The second ball I faced was a long-hop which I pulled for four. It's always nice to get off the mark so quickly, but this one brought up a significant milestone – 150, the halfway point.

Davey and I were feeling calm and confident together. He was dealing with Swann very well, and I got some overpitched balls from Anderson. In one over, I square-drove one ball for four, sent the next one down the ground, and made it 11 from the over when a low shooter came off the outside edge and ran through the slips. Davey hustled along and turned a two into a three – more good intent.

In the 44th over, we were 2/167. Swann and Anderson had both bowled for three-quarters of an hour since tea, and Cook decided to replace them both. From the Finchale end, Bresnan came on for Swann. I got his first ball away for a single. But three balls later, he sent down a cracker to Davey, one that was pitched well up, hit a lively spot and took off. Throughout the game there has been the odd ball that behaved this way, flying high and fast, unexpectedly, through to the keeper. Mostly it hasn't taken a wicket. This time it was just close enough to Davey to get the edge. He'd played a terrific innings, one of his best, and although he was obviously disappointed not to have batted all the way through, he'd got us close enough so that the middle order should have been able to finish the job. Going forward, it's great to see Davey batting like this.

Broad replaced Anderson at the Lumley end, and started off with a good straight yorker. There was all the usual by-play going on. My concern was not to be passive. I defended Broad's sixth ball down the wicket. He stuck his boot out, but it went past him. Even though it was only just running past the stumps at the other end, I saw the chance for a single and took off. It was tight, but I felt it was important for Smithy and I to let England know we weren't going to let them dictate the tempo of the game.

Just before the drinks break, England lost their second and last DRS referral. Smithy pulled at a short one from Broad, and umpire Hill ruled him not out, caught behind. The replay showed the ball to be hitting Smithy's hip, not his bat. You never know if these things are going to be significant later in the game, but the way things have turned out in this series, it could be an advantage for us that England could no longer ask for any reviews.

At drinks, we were 3/174: just 125 runs to go. It was a long last session, due to the rain break, with about 16 overs left in the day – far too early for us to think about whether or not we could press for a win this evening, so Smithy and I just stressed to each other to keep playing positively.

First ball after drinks, my innings came to an end. I got a good one from Broad, who, as I've said before, has the ability to get outswing with the reverse-swinging ball. It was angled in towards me, I played down the expected line, and it just tailed away a little, enough to beat the bat and clip my off stump.

As upset as I was at getting out, though, I had full confidence. Watto batted so well in the first innings, he had Hadds behind him, and Smithy has had an excellent series. There was no reason for pessimism.

Broad had upped his pace, however. He bowled that over, to me and then Watto, at a full 10 km/hour faster than at any other time in the series. He was harnessing his increased effort and pace to maintained accuracy and control. The light was fading, and he was going to be a handful.

In his next over, he bowled a short one to Smithy. Steve wasn't lucky: he played a pull shot, the ball was onto him a bit early, and it hit his arm. From there, it dropped down onto the stumps. So many times, from both sides, similar shots have resulted in the ball running away harmlessly. Not so for Smithy.

With two of our most experienced batsmen at the crease, we were well equipped to deal with the storm. But Watto and Hadds were both out LBW to umpire's call decisions. Watto moved across his stumps to Bresnan, and Hadds fell to Broad; the onfield umpires gave both decisions out, but the ball tracker showed both to be making some contact with leg stump. Hadds' one was particularly close to missing. As per the playing conditions for this series, the benefit of the doubt went not to the batsmen but to the onfield umpires. Their decisions stood. We were gutted, but those are the conditions we've agreed to, and it's the same for both sides. It's just hard to take when these sequences occur at moments when you're fighting your backside off to win a Test match.

Still, we never give up. Sidds, Ryan Harris, Nathan Lyon and Jackson Bird all believed they could survive the tough period, get us through to stumps and somehow conjure a win. For all the wickets that had fallen, we needed less than a hundred to win. It was doable. But we just couldn't build that vital partnership. At 7.30 pm, the umpires extended what was already a marathon session because they thought England had a realistic chance of winning. When the clouds closed in, they gave Cook the option to use his spin bowlers, so Swann and Joe Root came on. Then, when the sun came out again, they allowed him to use Broad and Anderson. In the end, it was Broad who dismissed a very, very disappointed Peter Siddle with a catch at mid-off.

Stuart Broad deserves a lot of credit for what happened. When good bowlers like that get on a roll, they're hard to stop. Just four or five overs of hard work, and we could have seen him off. A decent innings from me, and we would have won.

Our mood was bleak, to say the least. I felt totally wrung out with emotion. But our standards are high in all things, and we are not a team to give in to the temptation to really let our disappointment show. I sucked it up and

THE FOURTH TEST MATCH

went out on the field to make a concession speech for the crowd, then a television interview, and finally a press conference.

I dread these press conferences. It's not that the questioning is hostile. It's more that they're the same, almost every Test match. How does it feel to me to lose? What can we do from here? How can we avoid it happening again? Do we have the right players? And always, lately, there's been some record from the past that we're in danger of breaking – the bad kind of records, that is.

In answering, I'm honest, but there's nothing more I can give, no new insights. I paid credit to Broad for an exceptional performance. Any bowler who gets his tail up like that is going to be hard to stop, and we couldn't do it. Why? Well, it's not poor preparation. Today we turned up with the attitude that we're going to win this Test match. I can't ask any more of the boys. Their preparation is faultless. Rhino Harris picked up another cream blazer award as man of the match for his bowling, while James Faulkner, who is always keen, took the pink jacket for the 'one-percenters'.

At the press conference, I was asked if we should keep picking the same players, which is a bit unfair given that I'm not a selector. But I do believe we're picking the best players we have. 'You can't just drop someone,' I said, 'unless there's someone better to take his spot.' We know we have to rebuild, but it takes time. We're playing good opposition, the best in the world, and this is the painful way of picking up experience. The selectors picked the best squad for these conditions. You pick the squad, you keep the faith and try to get the best out of them. That's all there is. How many players do we have with 50-plus Tests' worth of experience, as England have? Only myself and Hadds – and, as I said in the press conference, you can't just go out there with two players. And even then, I look at my own performance. If I'd scored 75 runs today, we would have won the Test match. It's that simple, and I couldn't do it. I made 27 runs in this Test match, which is unacceptable.

One of the last questions, of course, pointed out that no Australian team has lost a Test series 4–0 in England, so how much of our thinking for The Oval would be geared towards avoiding that record? I told them I'm not thinking about avoiding 4–0. It has no part whatsoever in my preparation. My focus is on winning this Test match because I want to win a Test match. The fifth Test match is as important as the first four Test matches. That's all the motivation I need.

Tomorrow we're having a meeting to discuss where we're at as a team. I can't imagine feeling lower over cricket than I do right now.

Fourth Test
9 August 2013. **Riverside Ground, Chester-le-Street.**

England (first innings)

Batting		R	B	4	6	SR
AN Cook	lbw: Bird	51	164	5	0	31.10
JE Root	c: Haddin b: Watson	16	52	1	0	30.77
IJL Trott	c: Khawaja b: Lyon	49	60	7	0	81.67
KP Pietersen	c: Haddin b: Lyon	26	35	4	0	74.29
IR Bell	c: Harris b: Lyon	6	17	0	0	35.29
JM Bairstow	lbw: Lyon	14	77	1	0	18.18
MJ Prior	lbw: Siddle	17	58	2	0	29.31
TT Bresnan	not out	12	49	1	0	24.49
SCJ Broad	c: Warner b: Harris	3	12	0	0	25.00
GP Swann	c: Lyon b: Harris	13	18	3	0	72.22
JM Anderson	b: Bird	16	16	4	0	100.00
	Extras (1lb, 3w, 6nb, 5b)	15				
	Total 10 Wkts, 92.0 Overs	238		2.59 Runs/Over		

Bowling	O	M	R	W	Econ	SR	Extras
RJ Harris	19.0	3	70	2	3.68	57.0	(5nb)
JM Bird	22.0	9	58	2	2.64	66.0	
SR Watson	13.0	6	21	1	1.62	78.0	(2w)
PM Siddle	18.0	6	41	1	2.28	108.0	(1w, 1nb)
NM Lyon	20.0	7	42	4	2.10	30.0	

Australia (first innings)

Batting		R	B	4	6	SR
CJL Rogers	c: Prior b: Swann	110	250	14	0	44.00
DA Warner	b: Broad	3	7	0	0	42.86
UT Khawaja	c: Prior b: Broad	0	6	0	0	0.00
MJ Clarke	c: Cook b: Broad	6	18	1	0	33.33
SPD Smith	c: Prior b: Bresnan	17	34	3	0	50.00
SR Watson	c: Prior b: Broad	68	134	7	0	50.75
BJ Haddin	lbw: Swann	13	22	2	0	59.09
PM Siddle	c: Cook b: Anderson	5	21	0	0	23.81
RJ Harris	lbw: Broad	28	33	5	0	84.85
NM Lyon	lbw: Anderson	4	7	1	0	57.14
JM Bird	not out	0	7	0	0	0.00
	Extras (11lb, 1w, 2nb, 2b)	16				
	Total 10 Wkts, 89.3 Overs	270		3.02 Runs/Over		

Bowling	O	M	R	W	Econ	SR	Extras
JM Anderson	25.0	8	65	2	2.60	75.0	
SCJ Broad	24.3	7	71	5	2.90	29.4	(1w, 2nb)
TT Bresnan	19.0	3	63	1	3.32	114.0	
GP Swann	18.0	5	48	2	2.67	54.0	
IJL Trott	3.0	0	10	0	3.33		

England (second innings)

Batting		R	B	4	6	SR
AN Cook	c: Haddin b: Harris	22	37	3	0	59.46
JE Root	b: Harris	2	19	0	0	10.53
IJL Trott	c: Haddin b: Harris	23	29	3	0	79.31
KP Pietersen	c: Rogers b: Lyon	44	84	6	0	52.38
IR Bell	b: Harris	113	210	11	0	53.81
JM Bairstow	c: Haddin b: Lyon	28	65	6	0	43.08
TT Bresnan	c&b: Harris	45	90	6	0	50.00
MJ Prior	b: Harris	0	1	0	0	0.00
SCJ Broad	c: Smith b: Harris	13	7	3	0	185.71
GP Swann	not out	30	24	6	0	125.00
JM Anderson	c: Haddin b: Lyon	0	5	0	0	0.00
Extras	(5lb, 1w, 0nb, 4b)	10				
Total	10 Wkts, 95.1 Overs	330		3.47 Runs/Over		

Bowling	O	M	R	W	Econ	SR	Extras
RJ Harris	28.0	2	117	7	4.18	24.0	
JM Bird	20.3	6	67	0	3.27		
SR Watson	6.3	1	22	0	3.38		
PM Siddle	17.0	4	59	0	3.47		(1w)
NM Lyon	22.1	3	55	3	2.48	44.3	
SPD Smith	1.0	0	1	0	1.00		

Australia (second innings)

Batting		R	B	4	6	SR
CJL Rogers	c: Trott b: Swann	49	100	8	0	49.00
DA Warner	c: Prior b: Bresnan	71	113	10	1	62.83
UT Khawaja	lbw: Swann	21	35	3	0	60.00
MJ Clarke	b: Broad	21	27	3	0	77.78
SPD Smith	b: Broad	2	19	0	0	10.53
SR Watson	lbw: Bresnan	2	11	0	0	18.18
BJ Haddin	lbw: Broad	4	6	0	0	66.67
PM Siddle	c: Anderson b: Broad	23	48	2	0	47.92
RJ Harris	lbw: Broad	11	18	1	0	61.11
NM Lyon	b: Broad	8	10	2	0	80.00
JM Bird	not out	1	24	0	0	4.17
Extras	(5lb, 0w, 0nb, 6b)	11				
Total	10 Wkts, 68.3 Overs	224		3.27 Runs/Over		

Bowling	O	M	R	W	Econ	SR	Extras
JM Anderson	16.0	1	73	0	4.56		
SCJ Broad	18.3	3	50	6	2.70	18.5	
TT Bresnan	13.0	2	36	2	2.77	39.0	
GP Swann	18.0	6	53	2	2.94	54.0	
JE Root	3.0	2	1	0	0.33		

8

THE FIFTH TEST MATCH

Tuesday 13 August. **Gateshead.**

What's meant to be the last day of the Durham Test match is, unfortunately, a day off. I woke up very early, my mind racing, and went to the gym, where I trained hard to get some of the pent-up frustration out of my system.

Last night, the team and support staff got together for a couple of beers in the bar of the Hilton, where we've been staying in Gateshead. Our team manager, Gavin Dovey, ordered some pizzas, and the team were in reasonable spirits consoling each other. I wasn't drinking alcohol; it was the last thing I felt like. I went to bed early.

All night I was tossing and turning, rolling over a number of things in my head about how we could have gone about that run chase better. The fact that we're 3–0 down in the series is absolutely devastating. Before I got on a plane here, the goal was to win my first Ashes series as a captain, and my first as a player in England. I can't reconcile myself to what's happened. In Manchester, not winning back the Ashes was tough to deal with, but that feeling was eased a little bit by how well we played there. We came out of that match with some confidence, and truly felt that we would level the series. But now, losing the series is devastating. I feel sick in the guts, to be honest.

The washout in Manchester hurt, but this is a feeling I couldn't prepare myself for. I had no idea it would feel this bad, and so personal. Last night, I asked myself why I played the shot I played, why I hadn't contributed more runs. It wasn't a feeling of anger so much as devastation. But yes, I am angry at myself for not performing as well as I'd have liked.

I'm extremely hopeful that we will learn from these times and they'll make us a better group and better players. But the truth is I don't know. It seems like we're not learning. I'm a part of that. I've played 90-odd Test matches. Why wasn't I the one to get through that period?

But beyond that, I'm devastated and disappointed that we've let ourselves down with the bat again. If I want to face up to it, it's been happening for three or four years, about ten times in that period. I'm questioning why we're still making those mistakes from the great positions

THE FIFTH TEST MATCH

we've got ourselves into. I lay in bed asking myself: is it my captaincy, my leadership – am I not working with the boys enough? Are we not working hard enough on our defence? If we'd defended Broad for five overs, we'd have won this match. But we didn't.

At 4.00 pm this afternoon, we got together as an entire squad for a frank discussion about where we're at, how guys are feeling, how the batting unit in particular can get better. We discussed how in the Test matches at Trent Bridge, Lord's and Chester-le-Street we've lost a lot of wickets in clumps. Darren tried to focus on just the current series, not India or any time before he's started. That's good for the guys, but I can't help thinking about how far these collapses have stretched back into the past, over a period of three or four years.

Darren wanted to give a balanced measure of where we're at. We can't hide behind the fact that we've lost wickets in rushes that have cost us the Ashes, but at the same time, we've come really close to winning three of the four Test matches.

It wasn't a discussion dominated by Darren, though, or myself or anyone else. Senior and younger players alike expressed their views. It was really positive. We spoke about finding times through the game when the opportunity arises, the door opens, and how we can go through to the other side, take our chances. We discussed how the winning feeling doesn't just happen. It becomes a habit.

We talked a lot about confidence, and having faith in your teammates, whether it's your partner when you're batting with him in the middle, or the guys around you when you're in the field. We stressed that we have to believe more in each other – trust.

Blokes spoke their minds, which was the best thing. They talked about how they felt the opposition were trying to get them out, and how they were trying to combat that. Everyone was disappointed, but trying to get better.

For me personally, I think I'm doing it tough. We're all doing it tough. But I can feel the boys rallying, which I really appreciate. Everyone's looking after each other.

At moments like these, I think about the horizon: us getting better as a team and as individuals every day. There's a photo on my phone which shows waves smashing the sand in the foreground, but far away the horizon is calm. That's what I'm looking at. Every single day I see my dream and my goal, which is for us to be the number one team in the world.

I'm not taking my eyes off that.

Wednesday 14 August. Gateshead to Northampton.

Once again I got up at about 5.00 am, before anyone else, and went to the gym. Even though I 'slept' for

THE FIFTH TEST MATCH

eight hours, I woke up feeling as if I'd had about one hour's sleep. There's so much churning inside me. In the gym, I flogged myself, thinking that nobody else I'm competing against is out of bed and in the gym at this time of the day. The next time the chips are down, I'm going to make this count for something.

The optimistic side of me says we're only one win away from having our confidence back. That's the amazing thing about sport: it only takes one win. If we'd won the First Test, or the Third Test, it might not have meant we would win back the Ashes, but our attitude and mindset would be completely different. We'd be full of confidence coming into the next match. We were *so* close to winning in Nottingham and Manchester; if those last phases had gone our way, I do think we would be in a different headspace.

We're burning and hurting, and I think that will hold us in good stead for the future, when we do turn it around. It's going to taste that much better when we win. I've had ups and downs and know how much the downs hurt. But you need 'rock bottom' to realise how much you cherish playing Test cricket for Australia and remember how much you love winning.

Since our team meeting yesterday, I've spent a fair bit of time having one-on-one chats with individual players. I had a good chat with Watto today, and also a good chat with Sidds before he left the team to travel to London, where he's going to freshen up over the next few days. He wanted to know how he could help out, as a senior player. I've also spoken a lot to Brad Haddin. Everyone's wanting to do more to help. Everyone's getting out of bed each day thinking, 'How can I get better and how can I help the team?' The effort and positive attitude they're putting in almost makes it harder for me. I just keep returning to the sense of responsibility for letting them down with my batting, especially in the Fourth Test.

Today we're driving on the bus from Gateshead to Northampton, a four-hour trip, before recovery and rehab. As a team, we'll settle down in the quiet surrounds there and reboot.

Thursday 15 August. **Northampton.**

The will is there. You can see that in our training sessions every day. We all worked hard for three and a half hours, each getting what we could individually out of the session. I'd had a chat with Watto about combatting England's bowling plans, and we worked on that together in the nets. Mainly the objective is to try to hit the ball as straight as possible, intending to hit balls from middle stump through the 'V' between mid-off and mid-on, rather than square of the wicket. Everything's connected – if you try to hit too square, you're only using half the face of the bat rather than the full face, and you become an LBW risk. With Shane, it's just a matter of starting with that intent – hitting straight – and grooving the balance and strokeplay from there.

I concentrated on facing short-pitched fast bowling, and copped a few bruises – one on my back and one on my thumb. This afternoon, I've had some physio treatment and put some ice on both of the knocks. I'm not too worried, but will monitor how I pull up tomorrow.

I'm not playing in the match against the England Lions here. As Hadds has gone to London with Peter Siddle and Ryan Harris, Shane Watson will captain the team in the match here and I'll run the drinks and help the boys out in any way that I can. More than anything, I'm sitting the match out to give my mind a rest. The mental fatigue of the tour is only to be expected, and it's not a bad experience at all, but without the medicine of winning matches you certainly feel the mental weariness. We've agreed that my best preparation for The Oval is to give my mind a few days off.

Friday 16 August. **Northampton.**

There was a bit of rain early, delaying the start of the match against the England Lions. On another very dry wicket that looked like it was going to take plenty of spin, Watto lost the toss and the Lions decided to bat.

Cleverly, they decided to pick as many left-handers as they possibly could, opposite to the England Test XI.

We picked up seven wickets, which was a good result on a shortened day. Nathan Lyon had a good long bowl, and probed very hard, giving the batsmen a thorough examination. We put down a few chances, unfortunately for Nathan, but then we had some luck when Steve Smith came on late and took a couple of wickets with full tosses. It was good for the boys to get out in the middle after a few days of disappointment and soul-searching, and good for me to be the drinks waiter. I did what I could to help them in the middle, and also spent some time in the nets working on my batting. The sun came up today, against all expectations, and I began to feel better about the world.

Saturday 17 August. **Northampton.**

The rain bands had thickened overnight, and the ground here in Northampton was a pretty gloomy sight this morning. The boys were able to get in a bit of training before play started late, and the England Lions declared on their overnight score, giving us a total of 83 overs in the day's play for batting.

We didn't bat as well as we would have liked, and it was a bit of a lull in our preparation. Nearly all the boys made starts, but a couple of decent deliveries and some less than optimal shot selection stopped anyone from converting into a big score. Still, on the upside, plenty of guys got some batting practice.

Bad light took us off before the close, after 68 overs in our innings. Then it rained, which put an end to the match. We packed up and headed to London, checking back into the Royal Garden Hotel at Kensington. To be honest, I think many of our minds have already moved forward to the Fifth Test, and making a big push to finish the series with a win under our belt.

Sunday 18 August. London.

Today was a team recovery day, which I really enjoyed. I had a good night's sleep and feel mentally refreshed after missing the game in Northampton. We had an excellent training session this morning, concentrating on strength and fitness, and then I went out for lunch with Mark Nicholas, former player and now commentator with the Nine Network and Channel 5 here in England.

Over the past few years, I've had regular get-togethers with Mark. Being outside the group, and as an Englishman who spends a lot of his life in Australia, he brings a different perspective. One thing I can depend on is his honesty. He brings his playing and commentary experience to his observations of the game, and he's very constructive in his opinions about where we're at as a team. I feel I can trust him, and always take something useful away from our conversations.

Afterwards, I came back to the hotel for some physio treatment from Alex and a massage from Grant, then some room service with Kyly. It's been a good day, and I feel better than I have at any time since the end of the Durham Test match.

Monday 19 August. London.

Today was our first time together as a team at The Oval (now called the Kia Oval), which is a very impressive sight – a big ground by English standards, with stands and the famous gasometer towering high over the field. I was keen to take a look at the pitch, which looks quite good to me. It has a reputation for spinning, and it certainly did during our Test match here in 2009. But it looks very good – dry, but maybe not quite as dry as the pitches we've had in the other Test matches. There's a fairly dense mat of dry grass on it. As long as they don't mow that off between now and Wednesday, I reckon there will be a bit of help for the bowlers on day one, good batting conditions on days one and two, and then some spin and reverse swing from day three onwards.

The selectors have come up with a new combination for the Fifth Test, and informed each of the players at the

THE FIFTH TEST MATCH

end of our training session today. It will be announced at our team meeting tonight.

After training, Ed Cowan and his wife Virginia threw a birthday party in Hyde Park for their daughter Romy, who has turned one. A group of us went across the road from the hotel into the park to celebrate, and it was good to see so many of the squad and staff turn up – another little indicator of how strong our spirit has remained, in spite of the results. It was a special day for Romy, who is extremely cute, and for the Cowan family.

Tonight we're having dinner for Popeye, our bus driver, and his wife Suzanne. It's her birthday today, but unfortunately she has cancer and is struggling. Popeye – Geoff Goodwin, owner of the Goodwins bus company – has been our driver on all the tours of England I've taken since my first one-day series here in 2004, and is a huge supporter of the Australian cricket team. I'm really feeling for him at the moment, and it's nice that the entire team is going to celebrate Suzanne's birthday with the two of them. I was touched to see how thrilled Geoff was when we told him everyone was coming. These moments are precious.

Tuesday 20 August. London.

All of our preparation is complete, after a good training session at the Kia Oval and another look at the pitch.

I still think it will be good for a couple of days, before deteriorating later in the match.

On the centre of the ground, we had a half-hour meeting of senior players – myself, Brad Haddin, Shane Watson, Peter Siddle and Ryan Harris – with Rod Marsh and Darren Lehmann. It was stressed that now more than ever it's so important for the senior players to lead the way, on and off the field. It's been a long tour and in so many ways a disappointing one, and when that happens you can reach breaking point towards the end. As the five senior Test players in the team, we have to take hold of the situation.

We had our team announcement last night, and I've sorted out the batting order. I'm particularly excited for young James Faulkner, who is making his Test debut tomorrow. He's been one of the top wicket-takers in the Sheffield Shield for the last three seasons, as well as a more than capable run-scorer in the lower middle order. He's a real fighter as a cricketer. He's also a right-handed batsman, which will assist in our plan to neutralise Graeme Swann.

I'm sure James won't be sleeping too much tonight! Every time I've crossed paths with him, at training or at the hotel, I've been telling him not to expect too much sleep. He can't wait, and I'm pumped for him as well.

Including James means we're going into the match one specialist batsman short of the usual six. That means our top five batsmen have to dig deep and cash

THE FIFTH TEST MATCH

in if they get a start, ensuring they turn a 40 or a 50 into a big score. Obviously, it's something we've talked about for a lengthy period, but as always, there's only so much talking you can do. Everyone's very excited about this Test match, and we're feeling fit and keen and optimistic.

Wednesday 21 August. London.

Today was a fantastic day for us, continuing a trend in the series where we really have competed with England and dominated the last three Tests for significant periods. It was Shane Watson's day, of course, with his 176. It's hard to put into words how happy I am for him; I'm absolutely delighted. It feels like a lot of investment — by him into his own game, and by the whole group — is paying off.

We had a cap presentation when we turned up at the ground, Shane Warne presenting James Faulkner with his baggy green. Warnie's a big believer that if you're good enough to make the Australian team in the first place, there must be a lot you're doing well on the cricket field. So he was telling James to keep playing the way he had played to get here.

The day broke warm and sunny, and with such a good wicket with potential to break up later in the game, it was one of those tosses that felt important to win. I called heads again, and it came up for me. In terms of the conditions, probably Old Trafford and here have been the tosses you would really want to win, so I was relieved to be able to tell Alastair that we would be batting.

There was a fair bit of movement early in the day for Anderson and Broad. England had brought in two debutants, Chris Woakes and Simon Kerrigan, for Jonny Bairstow and Tim Bresnan, who has a stress fracture. A lot of us expected Chris Tremlett to come in as a straight seamer-for-seamer replacement, but the selection of a second spin bowler to support Graeme Swann suggests what England think the wicket is going to do. Like us, they have only five specialist batsmen now, so it will be incumbent on those specialists in both sides to make big runs.

Davey Warner couldn't get going early, but Watto joined Chris Rogers and they compiled another significant partnership, getting through two hours of batting when the ball was doing a fair bit. Chris was impressive yet again, digging in for a long time and patiently dealing with Swann. What set a great example was how Chris went to his defence and relied on it, without getting agitated even when he wasn't scoring runs. It's a five-day match; there's no rush.

Shane was in terrific touch from the start. There has been the technical work we've done over recent weeks, and the rebalancing he's done for himself, but more than

THE FIFTH TEST MATCH

that it's been a matter of giving him confidence. When I told him he would be batting at number three, I said that it was because we believe he's the best player of fast bowling in our team, we all know he's a fantastic player, and he's best suited at the top of the order, where he can settle in against the new ball before building up towards a big score. Sometimes, as I well know, the switch can be thrown just by some simple reassurance, to hear that you're a huge part of the team and everyone believes in you. Shane mightn't have scored as many runs as he would have liked earlier in this series, and will say he was overdue, but that's all behind us now. What matters today is that he's our number three batsman and finished the day with the first century scored by an Australian in that position since Shaun Marsh did it on debut in Sri Lanka in 2011.

I was in with Watto four overs after lunch, very excited to be batting with him and to support him as he moved towards his century. It was quite an eventful little time. Swann started off bowling around the wicket, and I was staying on the back foot to turn the shorter ones away behind square leg for a single to get off strike.

Broad was already on at the other end, and he started with the usual short stuff. He bowled one very good bouncer that hit my bat handle and popped up. By the time I realised where it was, it looked like it might land on the pitch and roll back onto my stumps. I hustled back, but it went just clear on the leg side.

A couple of overs later, Watto had his own trial against Broad. Another bouncer got through his attempted hook shot and hit him at the top of his neck, just behind his left ear. He fell down and pulled his helmet off. I ran down the wicket, very concerned that he'd been hit on the bone. He wasn't saying much, just trying to regather his bearings. Alex, the physio, and Peter Brukner, the team doctor, both ran out into the middle, as a sign of how serious it might be. They gave the spot a rub and a checking over, and fortunately figured out that the ball had hit Shane not on the skull but on the muscle just below. He had a mark and a bruise there, and felt like it was corked, but luckily was able to stay on and keep batting. He'd scored 91 runs at the time.

Broad was giving me a solid workout with the short ones, placing a man at short leg, another at a short leg gully, and two out deep on the leg side. I was just trying to tough my way through that little session with a mixture of ducking and fending and, when I saw the ball early enough, a couple of pull shots. It was difficult, but I felt I was doing all right and soon enough Broad was given a rest, replaced by Anderson at the Vauxhall end.

Meanwhile Swann was probing away from the Pavilion end. I was feeling reasonably comfortable overall, though he got one arm ball to slide past my outside edge. It was a struggle, but this is what we've talked about – weathering these patches and getting through to calmer periods on the other side.

THE FIFTH TEST MATCH

Watto was dealing with both Swann and Anderson very correctly, following the plan and playing straight. Earlier in the morning, he'd taken on the debutant bowlers, giving Woakes and especially Kerrigan a bit of tap, but what was most impressive was how well he played Swann – as confidently as anyone has throughout the series. His defence was tight, and he was constantly able to get off strike by turning balls forward of square leg with the spin. It was a classic number three's innings, to be able to adapt his tempo and tactics to changing situations. He wasn't afraid to take a backward step either, having a little bit of argy-bargy with Anderson when the bowler wouldn't move out of his way as he took a run.

Anderson was complaining to the umpire about that, but soon enough he had a smile on his face. He bowled me an inswinger which clipped my front pad flap and went onto my stumps. I guess on another day it might have fallen safely and I would be on my way, but today that wasn't to be.

Watto was on 98 at the time, but I was back on the players' balcony to see him complete his century about five or ten minutes after I was out. We all burst into cheers and made sure we were out in a visible area, every last one of us, so that he could see us demonstrate our support.

Steve Smith joined him and together they batted for the next three hours. Smithy played yet another of the good innings he has strung together at number five on this tour. It's amazing to think that after not being in the initial squad, forcing his way in through the Australia A tour, he has now played in all five Test matches and given us something every time. He played with more freedom and self-assurance today the longer he was out there, and clearly enjoyed being in the middle with Watto in such dominant touch.

Late in the day, England took the second new ball, three overs later than when it fell due. Watto was moving forward, completely untroubled, and looked set to get through to stumps and push on towards a really big score. You always need some luck when you bat for a long time, and he had it when Cook put down a slips chance and he got a successful DRS referral on an LBW decision; but both were after he had scored his century. He was less lucky in one of the last overs of the day when he hit a solid pull shot off Broad but was caught, low down, by Pietersen out on the rope behind square leg.

His 176 feels like a big moment for this team, as much as it is for himself. It's a really positive sign as we look to the future. Watto has the opportunity to own that number three position for a long time. I'm confident this is the start of a new phase in his career, onwards and upwards. He certainly deserves the reward after the hard work he's put in.

So it was a really good day for us on a wicket that wasn't easy. I feel that anything over 450 in our first innings puts us in a great position to press forward and win the Test match. There's still a lot of work required to get us there, though. I'm extremely hopeful that Smithy, after his near miss at Old Trafford, can go on and make his First Test hundred, and that the lower order can support him and put us into position to apply some real pressure with the ball.

Thursday 22 August. **London.**

Some annoying rain, light but persistent, kept us in the changing room until 2.30 pm. Now that we're in a strong position in the match, obviously we want as much play as possible to press it home. There's more rain forecast for the weekend, so we're already preparing for having to win the Test match in less than the standard five days. It's frustrating. Again!

Smithy and Sidds eventually got out there, with a good 80-plus overs left in the day, thanks to play being extended until 7 pm. With a score of at least 450 in our minds, we wanted Smithy to stay in for as long as possible and the other boys to support him.

Sidds was out early, after looking in pretty good form, but then Hadds came in and built a very good partnership with Smithy. Hadds is known for his attacking batting, but he has the straightest bat you can imagine in defence, and he was really knuckling down early in his innings to survive that first period against Anderson, who was getting some swing both ways.

The conditions were helping the seamers, so despite having picked two spin bowlers, Cook didn't give either Swann or Kerrigan the ball until 32 overs had been bowled today. Hadds scored a nice 30, and then the all-rounders helped Smithy out. James Faulkner put aside the nerves of his First Test innings to go and hit out for the team, playing with excellent positive intent and Mitchell Starc also played some nice shots, both scoring quickly as we positioned ourselves for a declaration. I asked the boys at tea to play positively and push it along, and that's exactly what they went out and did, Rhino capping it off with a swashbuckling 33.

It was definitely Smithy's day, though. He's copped a bit of stick through this series from the opposition, and it's great to see him stand up and play the way he's played, not just today but since the First Test match. He's come on in leaps and bounds since he first played for Australia, and even since the beginning of this tour. What people don't see from the outside is how hard he has worked on all facets of his game, whether it's at training or during the tour matches. His hundred today was awesome to watch: when he got down the wicket to Jonathan Trott and hit that beautiful lofted drive over long-on for six, we all knew where it was going. There was no heart-in-the-mouth stuff, and no nervous shot selection of the type that got him out at Old Trafford. It was a beautiful controlled shot, and what a great way to bring up the three figures. A great moment for Australian cricket, and also a credit to him.

I was also extremely pleased that he ended up not out. It can feel that you've done your job when you have made a maiden Test century under a lot of pressure in an Ashes match, particularly for a young guy – Smithy is the youngest Australian to make an Ashes century since Ricky Ponting – but he still had a job to do for the team, after tea, and he pressed ahead and did it.

We declared at 9/492. The second-last wicket fell with two balls left in the over. I felt that with Steve on strike, he could hit two boundaries off those balls, so I sent Nathan Lyon out. Smithy hit the first one pretty hard into a gap, but unfortunately could only make a single; he was cursing himself for getting off strike. As soon as that happened, I called them both in.

This left us 22 overs in the day to try to winkle out a couple of early England wickets. I hadn't wanted to declare earlier, for reasons of time as much as runs. If I'd done it earlier, we would have had to bowl for a long session, which would have worn our bowlers down a little and taken the sting out of them for tomorrow, but also taken more of the shine off the ball. With 22 overs, we still have a newish ball to start with afresh tomorrow.

Unfortunately, those wickets didn't fall in the last session. Yet again, I felt that we wasted the new ball a bit, not making Cook and Root play often enough.

When we put it in the right areas, around a fourth-stump line and relatively full in length, we were able to go past the edge. A wicket seemed only a matter of time. But we weren't consistent enough with getting the ball into that corridor, and the chances didn't come. Or if they did, things didn't break our way: for instance, James Faulkner, with his first ball in Test cricket, got the outside edge of Joe Root's bat, but the ball died in flight and fell a few metres short of the slips cordon. It probably carried a piece of news we didn't want: this pitch has no life.

The umpires took us off five overs before the scheduled close, due to failing light. We've got our work cut out taking 20 wickets to win the match, to be honest. The weather forecasts are threatening to curtail some of the days – but more than that, the pitch looks dead and flat. At least, though, our first innings has put us in a nice position from which to have a red-hot crack. Those innings from Watto and Smithy, and the support they got from other batsmen right down the order, have put us in a place where we feel we can apply some scoreboard pressure.

Friday 23 August. **London.**

Well, as expected, it was an extremely tough day for us. Not exactly unsuccessful, as we bowled well and took

THE FIFTH TEST MATCH

important wickets, but ultimately we didn't get the succession of breakthroughs we needed to force the issue in this Test match.

There was a hazy, warm sunlight over the ground when we started, boding pretty well for a full day's play. Due to the time lost yesterday, the umpires scheduled a minimum of 98 overs, and play extending to 7.00 pm. We were feeling optimistic that if we bowled well, we could dismiss England today and get the Test match moving along.

We opened with Peter Siddle and Ryan Harris, because I felt they were the two bowlers least likely to waste the ball, which was still new. They tried their best, but again weren't able to get the ball in the danger area often enough. Cook and Root played and missed a few times, but nothing much was happening for us. Our best chance was when Root pushed for a risky single; Chris Rogers' throw would have run Cook out if it had hit the stumps from quite close range.

Mitchell Starc came on after six overs at the Vauxhall end, and I went down to field at mid-off to offer him encouragement and advice. Each ball, I delivered the message to him to keep believing in himself. In the latter part of that first hour, Starcy and Rhino, who switched to the Pavilion end, worked up some excellent pace and were unlucky not to take wickets. Both were regularly topping 145 km/hour in speed and also putting the ball in dangerous places. It was so close at times. Cook popped a leading edge between two fielders on the off side, and Root edged one down just past his stumps. Rhino hit Cook absolutely plumb, but the umpire gave it not out on the grounds that he thought it had pitched outside leg stump. We talked about referring it for a while, and ultimately decided to roll the dice. We were dead-certain it was hitting the stumps, and there was only going to be a centimetre or two in it either way over where it had pitched. We used our referral, and unfortunately the replay showed that the ball had pitched maybe two centimetres outside the line. That was a shame, and two balls later Rhino ran in and hit Cook again, in front but a little high.

Our plans against Cook have worked well all series. After this terrific spell of bowling from both ends before drinks, it took just three balls after the break to get him out. This time it was the full-pitched ball outside off stump, luring him to drive at a ball he might have been better off leaving. A straightforward nick gave Hadds his 26th catch of the series.

We went hard at Jonathan Trott early. He was in good form early in the series, but didn't convert his starts into any big scores. I placed two attacking short mid-wickets and a man at leg gully. He had a couple of sketchy moments early. On his third ball, he fell across his stumps and just nicked the ball onto his pad, saving him from the LBW. An over later, Rhino dropped in a short one and Trott tried to pull it, but it went off his

THE FIFTH TEST MATCH

glove or forearm. Instead of lobbing to slip for a catch, it ricocheted into his helmet. An over or so later, Trott fended one off his ribs and it flew at catchable height just a metre or two wide of the leg gully. My hands went onto my head – how close these things can be.

At this stage we felt like we could set off a collapse. Starcy came from around the wicket and tested out Trott and Root with his pace and height. About 20 minutes before lunch, I made a double change, bringing on Nathan Lyon from the Pavilion end and Sidds from the Vauxhall end. We were building dot-ball pressure and the batsmen were struggling to find any kind of timing or rhythm. Sidds bowled very well and hit Root in front. The umpire gave it not out, going down the leg side, and we didn't refer it. But it was another of those line-ball decisions that haven't gone our way. The ball-tracker replay showed that it was hitting the leg stump, enough to make it umpire's call; so if it had been given out by the onfield official, that decision would have stood. It certainly was going to hit a lot more of the stumps than some of ours which have gone against us. But I can't dwell on that, I'll drive myself mad.

At lunch, England were 1/97, going along very slowly. James Faulkner started after lunch from the Vauxhall end, with Nathan Lyon settling in for a long spell from the Pavilion end. As with all the bowlers all day, they were tight, persistent and accurate and I couldn't have asked any more of them. Gazza was getting a few to jump and turn, and eventually Root paid the price, going down for a sweep shot and being tricked by the extra bounce, top-edging the catch to Watto at short fine leg.

Again, we were in it. Just a matter of capitalising on the new batsman's nerves. Nathan bowled an exceptional spell to Kevin Pietersen. What a change from when Pietersen thought Nathan was a spinner he could just charge down the wicket at and knock him out of the attack. Twice Pietersen pushed forward uncertainly, and edged onto the on side. The first time, it flew past Smithy's arms too quicky for him to grab it. I moved Smithy a bit deeper, and the second edge flew just fine of his outstretched dive. It was so frustrating, because Nathan really did have the better of Pietersen and deserved a wicket. Pietersen paid him what might be seen as a great tribute an over or so after that second edge: so desperate was he to get off strike, he pushed a ball to Davey Warner at mid-on and just took off, with no hope of making his ground. Had Davey's throw hit, Pietersen would have been out by about three metres. It just showed how unsettled he was by Nathan's tight line and the natural variation off the pitch.

Still, the crucial wicket wasn't coming our way. I gave Smithy a few overs as the old ball got very soft, but they didn't take any risks. You always hope that the flight a part-time leg-spinner gives the ball will induce a careless shot, but England were in a digging-in mood, even if that meant scoring runs at a snail's pace.

THE FIFTH TEST MATCH

We took the second new ball as soon as it fell due. England were scoring at a touch over two an over, and showing no urgency. Starcy took the new ball from the Vauxhall end, and his first delivery was a searing inswinger, a touch short of a good length, and it beat Trott, trapping him dead in front. He referred the decision to the DRS, hoping it might have pitched outside leg stump, but he was gone.

Starcy was bowling one of his best spells of the series. He always has the capacity to bowl wicket-taking balls, but his problem has been consistency. Now he was really getting it in the right areas ball after ball, and I don't know how Pietersen and the new batsman, Bell, were getting through.

At this stage there was a bit of verbal by-play between Ian Bell and David Warner. Pietersen stood up for Bell, which is part of what you do in a team, and I stepped up on Warner's behalf. The finer details of it are best left on the field, but none of it was at all unusual in such a competitive arena where players are always sticking by their teammates.

On both sides of tea, Starcy bowled an excellent spell with the new ball. Honestly, I couldn't be happier with how all the bowlers put in. It was a fantastic effort on a very flat, dead wicket. Obviously we'd have liked a few more wickets, but it wasn't from lack of endeavour.

The light was gradually fading – the sun had gone behind a milky cloud cover for most of the day – and Sidds attacked hard in the last session. Pietersen was not batting at all fluently, trying to tough it out, and was hit in front by Sidds when he was on 44. Again, in our desperation to take a wicket, we referred the not-out decision, and again it went against us, this time the replay showing that it had hit him outside the line. An over or so later, James Faulkner nearly had his First Test wicket when Pietersen went for a pull shot and under-edged it just past his off stump. We were always threatening. Just after that, when I brought Starcy on from the Vauxhall end, Pietersen jammed down on a yorker and edged it to Watto at first slip. It was clear to us that the ball had hit the ground first, then the edge, and gone to Watto on the full, but the umpires sought to look at a replay just to make sure. It went our way, and we had that precious wicket.

But to England's credit, they battled through. We watched closely and observed the qualities required to stop one wicket turning into a clump. That's what we've got to be like: determined, vigilant and skilful when new batsmen are at the wicket.

Late in the day, the game pretty much petered out, England losing all interest in scoring runs. I had to put spinners on at both ends, or else I would have risked the umpires taking us off, and Smithy and Gaz strung together a succession of maiden overs to Ian Bell and Chris Woakes.

Tonight, we sure know we've been through a day of Test cricket. Seven hours in the middle, a lot of persistence on our part, knocking at the door again and again, and England having a mixture of good luck and good batting to get through the day only four wickets down. Tomorrow we've just got to stick at it, keep on fighting, and hope that the pitch deteriorates some more. It will be a massive day for us: quick wickets to bowl England out, get in and bat, and try to set a target so that we can win this Test match. I just know how good that's going to feel.

Saturday 24 August. London.

The rain looks like it's killing another Test match in which we have a strong position. I'm very disappointed, given the state of the game.

As I opened my blinds this morning it was raining, and it didn't let up all day. When we got to the ground, the ground was well covered, and although there were brighter breaks occasionally, when they got the Super Soppers and other drying equipment out, eventually another shower came down. By 4.30 pm, the umpires had abandoned the entire day's play.

Although I would rather have been out in the middle, I did my best to make the most of the time off the ground. I did an hour and a half of batting practice in the indoor nets at the Kia Oval, where the facilities are excellent. There are certainly some areas of my game I need to work on. Afterwards, I had a long talk with Rod Marsh. As well as being a selector now, and involved with Australian cricket throughout my career, Rod was my coach at the Commonwealth Bank Cricket Academy back when I was a kid, and he knows my game very well. We had a good chat, very constructive, and he's left me with some things to work on.

The boys generally tried to keep themselves busy while waiting to see if something would happen. Some players from the one-day squad have arrived, and to prepare for the series they went down to the indoor nets and practised with white balls. Other Test players also got through some practice. Up in the changing rooms, some of the players sat around reading books on their Kindles, and others spoke about cricket and the different stages we're at in our careers. There was a lot of discussion about times we'd spent in our early days, our experiences with rep teams and generally everyone's journey leading to where we are now.

Whiling away a rainy day always leads to distractions, and soon enough our coach provided one. Darren Lehmann agreed to Veet his back – that is, apply a hot waxy cream that then gets peeled or washed off the skin, taking the hair with it. Peter Siddle was the brave comrade who volunteered to put it on him. Everyone else was finding it very funny – no more so than when Boof realised, as he was taking the cream off, that there were areas in the middle of his back that he couldn't reach.

THE FIFTH TEST MATCH

He ended up hopping into the shower to wash it off, and I had to help him wipe the last patches of hair away. Nobody realises how tough it is to be Australian captain!

That gave everyone something to laugh about for half an hour, but otherwise it was a grim and disappointing day. Losing so many overs hurts us a lot in the context of the game. We knew we had a day of hard work to prise out those England wickets and give ourselves a chance to win the Test match. Losing a full day is going to make life difficult tomorrow. But we won't give up. England are still 45 runs short of avoiding the follow-on. Our aim is to take the remaining six wickets quickly, then send them back in and have a crack.

It sounds unlikely, but in cricket anything can happen.

Sunday 25 August. **London.**

It's been an action-packed series, played in a very competitive spirit, and I guess it was appropriate that it should end with a long, action-packed day. I'm feeling pretty washed out now that it's all over, and I know there will be a lot said about my role in what happened in the final stages. So I'll start at the beginning and go through it all.

There was still some rain around when we got to the Kia Oval, which was a setback for us, because whatever slim chance we had of getting a result from this match would hinge on having enough time.

We were eventually on the field about half an hour late, with the forecast good for the rest of the day. A few of us wore black armbands to signal our condolences after the death of the father of Damian Mednis, the Queensland Bulls strength and conditioning coach, who I've come to know very well back home.

Our attack started out with Ryan Harris and Mitchell Starc, and the English batsmen immediately played in a much more aggressive manner than on Friday. Our clear aim was to take the last six wickets quickly and enforce the follow-on, and England set about scoring those runs to deny us the chance.

We only took one of those wickets before they reached the crucial 293. Rhino bowled a scrambled-seam ball at Chris Woakes, which he drove at and nicked to me at second slip. The ball came very slowly, another indication of how little pace there was in the wicket.

James Faulkner had a terrific morning. His First Test scalp was what has become the most prized England wicket, Ian Bell. The ball went down the leg side, Bell got a touch, and Brad Haddin took one of his best catches, a diving left-handed effort with the ball dying on him. James was very fired up and we were all thrilled for him. Hopefully it's the first of many.

Starcy got the next wicket, yorking Stuart Broad in the first over of his second spell. After that, Matt Prior and Graeme Swann got away from us a little bit, putting on a few more runs than was ideal, given the plans that were going around in my head. I was busily thinking of a way to get a result out of the match, even now. If we could just get enough quick runs to build up a good lead, we might leave ourselves with enough overs to get England batting and have a crack at bowling them out. It wasn't very likely, but I was thinking it through. It didn't help us that Prior and Swann were putting on these annoying late runs.

James Faulkner put an end to it, ultimately. Prior went for a big hit but skied it down the ground, and Starcy ran around to take an athletic diving catch. Then we put down Anderson behind the wicket, but next over Faulkner had him caught nicking, and finally he bowled Swann, giving him figures of 4/51 on debut. It was a pleasing result for a young guy who's been keen, hard-working and very competitive in his outlook from the beginning of the tour.

So when the English innings finished on 377, there were approximately 67 overs left to be bowled in the day, light and weather permitting. Our lead was 115. In my mind, if we batted with positive intent until the rescheduled tea time and put on around 120 runs, that would leave us 44 overs to bowl England out. It would require a great effort, but the pitch was deteriorating and anything's possible. The alternative – to play out the day and let the match peter out to a draw – didn't hold much appeal. We wanted to play for a win, and to put ourselves in another pressure situation so we could learn from it. And there was a full house in. It's good for cricket if they can see two teams trying to win a Test match – certainly better than watching things drift away without purpose.

So the plan was 20 overs, 120 runs. I asked Watto and Davey Warner to open, as they would in a Twenty20 fixture. They didn't have to go out and bash – just bat normally, but with the intent to score runs whenever the opportunity presented. They did just that, getting us off to a bright start after settling in for a couple of overs. They had to play for the team, put the collective objective first, and that meant taking some risks. Both played some good shots and then got out, and I put in James Faulkner and Brad Haddin to follow. Hadds didn't last, but James played in enterprising style again, doing exactly as we wanted. I went out at number five, still wearing the long-sleeved shirt I had been wearing in the field. Swann was getting plenty of turn, hitting me just outside the line, which set off an LBW appeal and a DRS referral, which they lost. What I'd noticed was that spin of that degree might be very helpful to Nathan Lyon later in the day.

We kept pushing the runs along, and I was quite happy with the result: 111 off 23 overs by tea. I took the chance to declare during the break, so the game wouldn't lose those two overs for the innings change. Our lead was 227, which was low enough to give

THE FIFTH TEST MATCH

England thoughts about going for the win off the overs that remained in the day. We wanted that to happen, because it might increase our chances of taking wickets. Wickets were all we had in mind.

Ryan Harris and Mitchell Starc opened our attack again, and I set attacking fields with as many as five catchers in the cordon. They bowled a few loose ones, and Alastair Cook and Joe Root showed their intent by taking the runs on offer. In the fifth over, Rhino had Root edging one. Hadds' catch was his 29th in the Ashes – overtaking Rod Marsh's world record, set 30 years ago, for dismissals in one Test series. It's a great achievement by Hadds and richly deserved. Being the perfectionist he is, he's not completely satisfied with his keeping throughout this series – he's had a generally excellent time, interspersed with a few ragged periods here and there – but the big picture is, he's come back into Test cricket after an 18-month absence, given a huge amount to our team on and off the field, and been a terrific team leader. The world record is the icing on the cake. I know he would trade it for winning the Ashes and grabbing every single chance that came his way and not letting through a single bye, but overall his wicketkeeping has been impeccable, and his experience invaluable.

England were pressing forward, and Trott and Cook batted with plenty of intent. They weren't lashing out, but I could see they were trying to get to a point where they couldn't lose the game, by keeping wickets intact, before deciding whether or not to have a real run at the target.

As at Old Trafford, I decided to give myself a bowl just to see if it created a change in the game. With luck, the batsmen might take a risk against me and lose a wicket. But they treated my two overs with plenty of respect – maybe too much respect! – and as a wicket didn't fall, I took myself off again.

England were keeping up a run rate of about four an over, and the required rate was in the high fives. We got a breakthrough when James Faulkner had Cook LBW, but with 25 overs left to be bowled it was kind of a mixed blessing. We wanted wickets, of course, but Cook's dismissal brought in Pietersen, potentially a much more destructive batsman. Still, we had to take those wickets.

Pietersen was immediately on the attack, such a contrast from the way he batted two days ago. Some of our bowling was a little too short, and when he's in that mood he takes a full toll. I was still setting attacking fields, but when England got within 100 runs of the target, we were leaking runs a bit too easily. We still wanted to take those eight wickets, but the better tactic now seemed to be to try to frustrate the batsmen into taking more risks. So I dropped a couple of fielders back, put in a third man, and brought on Watto and James Faulkner to tie things up. They are probably our most experienced Twenty20 'death' bowlers, and

THE FIFTH TEST MATCH

we thought it might be worth a mix of slower balls and limited-overs-style bowling to search for the vital breakthrough.

Watto and James did give them cause to think and slow down a little. Then I brought back Ryan Harris from the Pavilion end. By now he was struggling with some hamstring soreness after all the bowling he's done, but as usual he was willing to bowl through the fatigue and pain. His first ball, Pietersen came down the wicket and tried to hoist him over the wide long-on boundary. He got under it, and Davey Warner ran around to his right to take a very well-judged catch.

This opened the door for us again, and in the next over James Faulkner had Trott out LBW. We had a definite chance. England needed 57 runs to win, but had two new batsmen, Ian Bell and Chris Woakes, at the wicket. There was a possibility they might go for the runs and take risks. We only had eight overs left, but I was still thinking about how we could win.

Rhino finally succumbed and had to go off. All of our bowlers were very tired. Bell and Woakes took advantage, and after a brief lull started to hit a few fours and get within striking distance. I still thought we had a good chance of winning.

At this point, I had no intention of giving England any gifts. Starcy bowled from the Vauxhall end, and Bell and Woakes were getting into full flow. The light, which I hadn't thought about too much, was very bad now and we were throwing sharp shadows from the floodlights. There was pretty much no natural light and it was akin to playing in a day–night match. A ball was hit out onto the leg side, and Peter Siddle, fielding at deep square leg, ran around with his hands in the air, not knowing where it had gone.

I approached the umpires a couple of times asking if the light was worse than when we'd been sent off at other times in the series. The crowd wasn't very pleased when I asked the umpires if they had their light meter. I can see they were a partisan group and wanted England to win – but again, it's not incumbent upon us to give it to them. All the umpires have to do in that situation is apply the rules consistently. They have taken us off the field on several occasions throughout this series when they judged the light unsafe for play. I haven't always agreed with them, but I've had to accept their rulings.

For some reason, it was taking some time to have the light meter brought out. It was a good deal darker than when we'd been taken off on Friday afternoon, and there was no comparison to Old Trafford, when they'd stopped us batting although we were in no fear for our safety.

On the last ball of the 40th over, Bell drove Starcy back down the wicket. Mitchell stuck his foot out and trapped the ball, picked it up, threw it at the striker's end and ran Bell out. Our first run-out of the whole series, would you believe!

THE FIFTH TEST MATCH

At that point, England needed 21 runs to win, and we needed five wickets. Four overs remained. It was the darkest we've played, by some distance. The light meter was brought out, and Aleem Dar held it up to read it. He pushed me away with his hand on my chest, saying, 'Go away, go away,' and I pointed out to him that I didn't want him touching me. If I touched him, I'd face a suspension for several matches, so it was only fair that he kept his hands off me as well. The whole situation only lasted for a few seconds, but I felt I had a right to be part of the discussions. It's the umpire's decision, of course. But at Old Trafford, Tony Hill and Marais Erasmus had consulted with the fielding captain when they were considering the light, and I was only asking for the same courtesy here.

In any case, as was pretty obvious, the meter showed that the level of light was several degrees darker than at other stages in the match when the teams had been sent from the field, so the umpires did the only thing they could and told the teams we were going off. As it was now 7.36 pm, the rules also stopped play resuming.

So the match, and the series, was over.

Off for bad light, no result.

The crowd voiced their frustration. All I can say is that the players were frustrated too. When we walked off, I still believed that we could have taken five wickets in the remaining 24 balls.

Getting booed as we walked off was not a nice feeling, especially when we've done everything in our power to set up the Test match. That was hard for the boys to hear and experience. But once we were inside and had five minutes to talk about it, everyone was convinced it was too dark to keep playing. It was a no-brainer. When we sat down, we couldn't believe we'd been booed, but then that's part of playing away from home.

We went into the England changing room to shake hands with each of their players, as a team, and congratulate them on their series win.

Out on the field, when England received the Ashes, the disappointment of the whole series hit us. Through my experience of winning and losing the Ashes, seeing the other team presented with the urn and celebrating with it is the moment when the devastation sinks in. That was a tough time for the team, but it's part and parcel of not winning, to stand there and watch that. I don't believe you can turn your face away from it. It's not a nice feeling, but you have to take it and use it to fuel yourselves. I hope it motivates us for what's around the corner.

We thanked the Australian fans at the ground for their support, and went back into the changing room for half an hour. I had to do media on the field and in the indoor nets where the press conferences were held. I felt I'd said everything I could say. I was out of words. We'd lost 3–0. I just wanted to give credit to England for their win, and to our boys for their work ethic.

After chatting in our changing room, we decided it would be a good time to go into the England room and have a beer with them and say well done. All of our boys went in, which I feel is important when you lose. I saw Cooky first, shook his hand and congratulated him, and then spent some time talking with Matt Prior and Graeme Swann. We stayed for about an hour. Before I left, I went to each England player, shook hands individually, and congratulated them on winning a tough series.

We stayed in our changing room for another 45 minutes, then went back to the team hotel in Kensington, where we showered and changed and all met at the bar. Shane Watson was wearing the cream blazer for man of the match at the Kia Oval, and Nathan Lyon was in bright pink for the one-percenters. I stayed at the bar for a while, then invited whoever was still there back to my room, where we had another drink. The mood was mixed – relief that the series was over, disappointed in the final result, but optimistic that we can turn things around in a few months.

Monday 26 August. **London.**

After a few hours sleep, I got up to say goodbye to the Twenty20 players, who caught a bus to Southampton to get ready for their first match on Thursday. I sat on the bus with them for about 15 minutes, having a chat. Then I rested up in the hotel and emerged again in the afternoon to spend some time farewelling the players who are flying home to Australia this evening. Phillip Hughes and I, being the two one-day players who are not in the Twenty20 team, are staying in London, before meeting up with the rest of the squad for the beginning of the one-day series next week.

Our Ashes tour is over! It's hard to know what to say. Over the past 24 hours, I've talked with all the players, but paid special attention to the younger ones, whose first Ashes tour this has been. I thanked them for their effort and asked how they'd felt on their first Ashes tour. To a man, they have shown excitement at having done it, and motivation for turning this result around in Australia in the coming months.

We talked a lot about what's happened and where we have to improve. There was disappointment, of course, but a lot of excitement about having the rare chance to turn it around so soon.

And I absolutely believe that we will. All of the players in this series have a little more experience under their belts. Importantly, we have exposed some weaknesses in the opposition, as we have proven at various stages of the series when we have been well on top. The secret – as always – is going to be converting those periods of dominance into victories.

I know we have the talent, the determination and the will.

As a team, we have plenty of fire in the belly.

Fifth Test
21 August 2013. The Oval, Kennington, London.

Australia (first innings)

Batting		R	B	4	6	SR
CJL Rogers	c: Trott b: Swann	23	100	3	0	23.00
DA Warner	c: Prior b: Anderson	6	11	1	0	54.55
SR Watson	c: Pietersen b: Broad	176	247	25	1	71.26
MJ Clarke	b: Anderson	7	39	0	0	17.95
SPD Smith	not out	138	241	16	2	57.26
PM Siddle	b: Anderson	23	27	2	0	85.19
BJ Haddin	b: Trott	30	57	5	0	52.63
JP Faulkner	c: Trott b: Woakes	23	21	4	0	109.52
MA Starc	b: Swann	13	8	1	0	162.50
RJ Harris	c&b: Anderson	33	27	1	2	122.22
NM Lyon	not out	0	0	0	0	
	Extras (12lb, 2w, 5nb, 1b)	20				
	Total 9 Wkts, 128.5 Overs	492		3.82 Runs/Over		

Bowling	O	M	R	W	Econ	SR	Extras
JM Anderson	29.5	4	95	4	3.18	44.8	(1w)
SCJ Broad	31.0	4	128	1	4.13	186.0	(4nb)
GP Swann	33.0	4	95	2	2.88	99.0	
CR Woakes	24.0	7	96	1	4.00	144.0	(1w)
SC Kerrigan	8.0	0	53	0	6.63		(1nb)
IJL Trott	3.0	0	12	1	4.00	18.0	

England (first innings)

Batting		R	B	4	6	SR
AN Cook	c: Haddin b: Harris	25	88	3	0	28.41
JE Root	c: Watson b: Lyon	68	184	11	0	36.96
IJL Trott	lbw: Starc	40	134	2	0	29.85
KP Pietersen	c: Watson b: Starc	50	133	4	0	37.59
IR Bell	c: Haddin b: Faulkner	45	143	5	0	31.47
CR Woakes	c: Clarke b: Harris	25	70	5	0	35.71
MJ Prior	c: Starc b: Faulkner	47	57	8	0	82.46
SCJ Broad	b: Starc	9	16	1	0	56.25
GP Swann	b: Faulkner	34	24	5	1	141.67
JM Anderson	c: Haddin b: Faulkner	4	10	1	0	40.00
SC Kerrigan	not out	1	12	0	0	8.33
	Extras (10lb, 5w, 3nb, 11b)	29				
	Total 10 Wkts, 144.4 Overs	377		2.61 Runs/Over		

Bowling	O	M	R	W	Econ	SR	Extras
MA Starc	33.0	5	92	3	2.79	66.0	(2w, 2nb)
RJ Harris	28.0	10	64	2	2.29	84.0	(1nb)
JP Faulkner	19.4	3	51	4	2.59	29.5	
PM Siddle	28.0	7	74	0	2.64		(1w)
NM Lyon	28.0	8	59	1	2.11	168.0	
SPD Smith	8.0	3	16	0	2.00		

Australia (second innings)

Batting		R	B	4	6	SR
DA Warner	c&b: Anderson	12	28	2	0	42.86
SR Watson	c: Pietersen b: Swann	26	32	2	1	81.25
JP Faulkner	c: Prior b: Broad	22	22	0	1	100.00
BJ Haddin	c: Prior b: Broad	0	1	0	0	0.00
MJ Clarke	not out	28	28	3	0	100.00
SPD Smith	c: Swann b: Broad	7	12	0	0	58.33
RJ Harris	b: Broad	1	2	0	0	50.00
MA Starc	not out	13	13	2	0	100.00
CJL Rogers						
PM Siddle						
NM Lyon						

Extras (2lb, 0w, 0nb, 0b) 2
Total 6 Wkts, 23.0 Overs 111   4.83 Runs/Over

Bowling	O	M	R	W	Econ	SR	Extras
JM Anderson	6.0	1	27	1	4.50	36.0	
SCJ Broad	10.0	2	43	4	4.30	15.0	
GP Swann	7.0	0	39	1	5.57	42.0	

England (second innings)

Batting		R	B	4	6	SR
AN Cook	lbw: Faulkner	34	53	4	0	64.15
JE Root	c: Haddin b: Harris	11	17	2	0	64.71
IJL Trott	lbw: Faulkner	59	87	6	0	67.82
KP Pietersen	c: Warner b: Harris	62	55	10	0	112.73
IR Bell	run out: Starc	17	17	1	0	100.00
CR Woakes	not out	17	13	1	0	130.77
MJ Prior	not out	0	0	0	0	
SC Kerrigan						
SCJ Broad						
GP Swann						
JM Anderson						

Extras (4lb, 0w, 2nb, 0b) 6
Total 5 Wkts, 40.0 Overs 206   5.15 Runs/Over

Bowling	O	M	R	W	Econ	SR	Extras
RJ Harris	5.0	0	21	2	4.20	15.0	(1nb)
MA Starc	7.0	0	48	0	6.86		(1nb)
PM Siddle	3.0	0	16	0	5.33		
NM Lyon	10.0	0	44	0	4.40		
MJ Clarke	2.0	0	4	0	2.00		
JP Faulkner	8.0	1	47	2	5.88	24.0	
SR Watson	5.0	0	22	0	4.40		

9
CONCLUSION

As a way of rounding this diary off, I thought it might be helpful to discuss some of the issues and controversies that went on during the tour. Most of my views emerged through the helter-skelter of events as they happened, but now that the tour is over, I can organise my thoughts and reflect on the incidents.

David Warner

Davey knew he let the team down when he had that altercation with Joe Root in Birmingham. It disrupted our preparations for the Ashes and the Champions Trophy, and cost him his place in the Test team at Trent Bridge and Lord's. The most important thing was for him to recognise the effect his actions had had on the whole team, as well as on himself.

He took his punishment and went away to Africa, where he made a fantastic 193 for Australia A. When he came back into the team, he was welcomed with open arms. His work ethic was outstanding and he made a few runs, highlighted by his second innings at Chester-le-Street. I was pleased with the way he came back in and with the way the others accepted him. He knew he'd let them down and had to earn their respect, and I think he did that.

The coach

It was difficult for all of us to accept that 18 days before an Ashes series, our coach was sacked. That was my biggest fear: that the decision, whatever its merits, would adversely affect our preparation.

What made it easier to take was that the replacement was Darren Lehmann. That's as good as you can ask for, by way of a new coach. Darren's a great guy and he's been fantastic as head coach. He deserves a lot of credit for the good things that have happened on this tour. We haven't had the results we'd like, but we've stuck together on and off the field, which will stand us in good stead going forward. It's team first now.

An unusual thing about this team is that we started badly and got better. Often, teams that lose Test series on long tours gradually disintegrate, as the disappointment catches up and causes fragmentation. In our case, we are definitely a stronger unit now than when we came to England.

A lot of players had a change of attitude when Darren took over the coaching role from Mickey Arthur. As hard as it was at the time, the change of coach ultimately had a positive effect on the team's performance.

The DRS

I believe in technology. When I look at how technology has improved the adjudication of run-outs and stumpings, I think we're lucky to live in this era. I'm all for improving the game, and technology has the potential to do that.

My concern is that the technology in this series hasn't been as consistent as it needs to be. If you're using technology, it has to be bulletproof.

Umpires, just like players, make mistakes in the heat of the moment. Test cricket is a tough game to play and I'm sure it's a tough game to umpire. My view on technology is fairly simple: it's there to take out the 'howlers', to assist the onfield umpires when they haven't been able to make a decision, or when they've got something badly wrong.

What's the best way to do this? I think we've seen a couple of problems arise in this series. One is human error by the third umpire. The one that comes to my mind is the decision to give Usman Khawaja out in the first innings at Old Trafford. When the third umpire has plenty of time to make his decision, he needs the training and help to act correctly.

The next troublesome area has been when the technology has caused mistakes. Sometimes this has been where Hot Spot hasn't shown an edge; sometimes it's a combination of factors. My opinion is that if the technology isn't perfect, it shouldn't be used at all. The inventor and owner of Hot Spot came out and admitted it doesn't pick up all nicks. Okay, that's fine: Hot Spot should not be used until it is more reliable. I can see why India don't like to use it – because they don't believe it's 100 per cent correct. Once the technology has been tested and is shown to be correct, then the ICC should rule that every team has to use it. We should have the same rule for everyone.

Finally, the referral system – where captains have two unsuccessful referrals at their disposal – can distort the process. I don't like the tactics involved, where umpires and the teams know how many referrals are left, and change their decisions accordingly. It should be consistent for all players. The ultimate problem with the Broad 'dismissal' in Nottingham wasn't that he didn't walk, or that the umpire had made an error – it was that the complicated DRS rules meant the third umpire didn't have the opportunity to overrule the onfield decision.

CONCLUSION

I believe that if it's clearly shown that the batsman hit the ball and he was caught, then the technology should be used to ensure he is out. If he's hit in front of the wickets and the technology shows he is LBW, he should be out, regardless of how many referrals remain.

As a captain, I'd just like the technology to be used to make more correct decisions, without all the complications of how many referrals remain or don't remain. There shouldn't be a numerical limit. If this means passing referrals back into the hands of the three umpires, on and off the field, then so be it.

My final word on the matter – if technology, and the use of that technology by umpires, continues to be as inconsistent as it has been in this series, I would rather it is not used at all.

(Interestingly, as I write this conclusion, the ICC has recently made a change to DRS, giving each team two additional reviews after the 80th over.)

Our batting order

It's been widely remarked that our batting order changed a lot during this series. I would love our batting order to be as consistent as possible – but when players are not performing, the selectors will make changes and that affects the batting order. Then there's the influence of conditions in each match, and the opposition's tactics.

We changed our order to use the left-handers up the top and the right-handers in the middle, which we've seen work, in patches, in the second half of the series. Like everybody else I'd like to know our top seven automatically, but we batsmen have to earn that with performances. You earn the right to a stable position by scoring runs.

Part of playing the game is adapting, and batsmen have to do it as much as bowlers do. I'm pleased to say that our team have accepted that we're doing everything we can to win the game. In the second innings at the Kia Oval, I had to tell Chris Rogers that he'd be going down the order because we needed to attack for 20 overs. He accepted and agreed with it. Other players accepted and agreed with changes throughout the Test matches.

That said, a more settled order has been taking shape through the series, as players have started to perform. But there will always be times when we need to adapt to the match situation.

Aggressive declarations

I've been questioned by a number of people about my decision on the last day of the Fifth Test to set up the game for a potential result. There has been some criticism that I gave England too much of a chance.

But this is the way I've been brought up to play. You risk losing in order to win. We certainly risked losing that Test, but we play the game to try to win, and we hope to entertain people along the way. I know the players enjoy that brand of cricket; they've made it clear to me, time and again. Personally, I don't know any other way, and I think that's what has got me to where I am. And it's the Australian way. We only have eyes for winning. We draw or lose only when we can't win.

If Cricket Australia want me to be captain, that's the way I'll play. If I'm not the right man, I'll accept that.

Captaincy and batting

There's no doubt I wanted to make a lot more runs than I did in this series. I scored nearly 400 runs at an average of just under 50, so it certainly wasn't my worst series, but with one century and one 50, I am disappointed that I didn't play more match-changing innings when it mattered. I got a couple of good balls, I played a couple of bad shots, I played a couple of good innings.

As captain, I expect myself to lead the way with runs. It can't always happen, that's the game, but I'm continuing to try to improve my game before the Australian summer. I feel the same every series. I know the Ashes is the pinnacle for an Australian cricketer, but my expectation for my performance is the same whether I'm playing England, South Africa, India or anyone else. I go to training every day of my life with the same focus, whatever the opposition. I just want to become the best player I can be. I've worked as hard through this series as in every other one, and haven't got the results I've wanted, but I have faith that I'll turn it around.

But batting is only one part of captaincy. I didn't know what leading an Australian tour to England was going to be like, because I was so focused on taking it as another opportunity for our team to develop towards its goal of being number one in the world.

What I've realised, more and more, is that as captain you feel accountable for everyone in the group. As a young player, you might be trying to hold your place in the team, and if you win, you might still feel bad if you haven't made a personal contribution. As a captain, *everything* is personal. So I've felt the sting of losing a lot more deeply. But more than that, my overriding emotion is sympathy for the boys who've put in so much work, to not have some Test wins. I feel really bad on their behalf that we've lost the series.

The other side of that coin is that, as captain, your best days are when your teammates do well. I've spent a huge amount of energy helping the other boys on this tour, and the most pleasing days are when they have succeeded. I'm thrilled that Chris Rogers and Steve Smith made their first Test hundreds and that Watto made his highest Test score, a big 176. I've been delighted that David Warner has worked so hard to win back the team's respect. The batsmen who have lost their places — Ed Cowan, Phillip Hughes and Usman Khawaja — have impressed me no end with their work ethic and positive demeanour. We need to make a lot of runs in Australia, so it's important for us to keep this going.

For the rest of the team, I see them as the heroes of the tour: Hadds for his consistently good wicketkeeping — rewarded with a world record — and team-focused batting, Matty Wade for always working hard and backing Hadds up; and the bowling group as a whole, led by Peter Siddle and Ryan Harris, with James Pattinson, Mitchell Starc, Jackson Bird, Nathan Lyon, Ashton Agar and James Faulkner — all of them doing their part for their team and country. Ryan was deservedly our man of the series, but in accepting that award he was also standing there representing the Australian bowlers as a group of men.

I always enjoy the privilege of playing for Australia, and of being our captain. This tour has had its full share of highs and lows. But as I've said, when I'm in any doubt, I think of those waves battering the shore and beyond them, the calm and peace in the distance.

My eyes remain on that horizon.

Acknowledgements

Just like playing cricket, writing a book is a team effort. Thanks to the Macmillan crew who have been exceptionally professional, and to Jim for helping me pull all the elements of the diary together.

Big shout out also to my teammates – a great and talented bunch of guys and a pleasure to captain.

Finally, thanks to my wife, Kyly, who puts up with the life of a professional sportsman with grace and good humour.